Being the Church in an Age of Offense

SUZANNE D. WILLIAMS

Being the Church in an Age of Offense
by Suzanne D. Williams
www.suzannedwilliams.com

Published by Becky Combee Ministries, Inc.
www.beckycombeeministries.com

ISBN-13: 978-1-7350401-0-3

All CAPTILIZED words are at the author's discretion and are meant to bring attention to certain words and phrases.

Any footnotes written in parenthesis with either *G + number* or *H + number* (ex.: G25) are references to the Greek or Hebrew definitions of a word or phrase as given in Strong's Hebrew and Greek Dictionary, as it is provided through e-sword Bible software. www.e-sword.net

Similarly, any references to commentaries such as Vincent's Word Studies and Thayer's Greek Definitions, or any other named work is taken from e-sword Bible software.

All scriptures are in King James Version unless otherwise noted as follows.

"The realm of heaven's kingdom is bursting forth, and PASSIONATE PEOPLE have taken hold of its POWER." (Matthew 11:11 TPT)

Table Of Contents

Foreword

"All scripture is given by inspiration of God ..." (2 Timothy 3:16)

The Bible is an amazing book. Sixty-six chapters, penned by forty authors, over thousands of years, compiled in one binding. Words written in three languages: classical Hebrew, Aramaic, and Koine Greek.

Words that have incited rebellion and caused imprisonment and death. To say this book has caused controversy is to speak lightly. The most commonly read version, the King James, has a storied history, not all of it godly. William Tyndale, who is responsible for translation from the Hebrew and Greek texts into English (instead of Latin), years before then, paid for the rebellious act with his life. No one wanted him to do it.

But he said, speaking to those who stood against him: "If God spare my life ere many years, I will cause a boy that driveth the plow, shall know more scripture than thou dost."

Author David Teets said of Tyndale in his book about the man that he had "magnificent backbone." I submit that for him and others like him, it was far more than that.

It was inspiration of God.

The phrase *"inspiration of God"* is more properly translated "God-breathed," but I like what *Thayer's Greek Definitions* gives as its origin.[1] The word comes from two other words: *Theos* or the Godhead, the Trinity, "refers to the things of God, his counsels, interests ... whatever can be

---

[1] G2315

in any respect likened unto God, or resemble him in any way"[2] and *pneo*, a word meaning breathe or blow.[3]

These words that men were inspired to write are like God. They resemble Him, His counsels, His interests. This is marvelous to me.

The J.B. Phillips translation of this verse gives it additional meaning.

"All scripture is inspired by God and is useful for teaching the faith and correcting error, for re-setting the direction of a man's life and training him in good living. The scriptures are the comprehensive equipment of the man of God and FIT HIM FULLY for all branches of his work." (2 Timothy 3:16-17)

Only the Bible has been required to define itself. Only the Bible inspires its believers to radically change their lives. In its pages is the breath of God that will set the direction of a man's life, making him fully fit, completely equipped, for anything he needs to do and everything he must face. These words are the fuel of the PASSIONATE church. They are the POWER OF GOD unto salvation.[4]

It is not separate authors from differing years tossed together by religious zealots nor separate books of differing ideas, each with their own separate stories. I believed that as a child. But, no, what makes this book, these verses, so dear to so many, is that from Genesis to Revelation, it tells one story. One fantastic God-breathed story of a love so great it would sacrifice its very best to save people who didn't deserve it.

It is the story of Jesus Christ, the Anointed One, the

---

[2] G2316
[3] G4154
[4] Rm 1:16

Messiah. A story of miracles, of signs and wonders. It is a commission to share its truths and an incredible ZEAL to everyone who believes.[5]

"Then said Jesus unto him, Go, and do thou likewise." (Luke 10:37)

Here is our calling. With these words, we become THE CHURCH, but not out of rote or formula. No! We do what Jesus did, we act like Jesus, we imitate Christ, staying full of the Holy Spirit.[6] His FIRE burns in us, giving proof of God's glory with SIGNS following.

"But when I tell myself, I'll never mention Your name or speak for You again, it's no use. The word of God burns in my heart; it is like fire in my bones. I try to hold it all in, but I cannot." (Jeremiah 20:9 VOICE)

This is what those outside of our Christian faith always fail to grasp. These words hold life that changes hearts, heals bodies, and restores minds. They are compassion when you most need it, strength when you're at your absolute end, encouragement and hope and faith to keep pushing forward. They are a compulsion to fulfill God's promises, a boldness that cannot be explained.

They are a light that no man can ever put out.[7]

---

[5] Ps 69:9

[6] Eph 5:1

[7] Jn 1:5 PHILLIPS

Chapter 1

The Passionate Bride

The bride stands outside the chapel, trembling with anticipation. Her face aglow, she takes a harried breath, his name upon her lips. Her heartbeat pounding, she leans in, straining to hear his footsteps. The bridegroom is near.

"And the Spirit and the bride say, Come." (Revelation 22:17)

The apostle Paul describes Christ and the church with the unity of husband and wife. This passage in Ephesians 5 is particularly moving in the Passion Translation where Christ's heart for the church is beautifully penned.

"And to the husbands, you are to demonstrate love for your wives with the same tender devotion that Christ demonstrated to us, his bride. For he died for us, sacrificing himself to make us holy and pure, cleansing us through the showering of the pure water of the Word of God. All that he does in us is designed to make us A MATURE CHURCH FOR HIS PLEASURE, until we become A SOURCE OF PRAISE TO HIM—glorious and radiant, beautiful and holy, without fault or flaw." (Ephesians 5:25-27 TPT)

How moving that is. It isn't the only reference to the church as the bride. We find it in Revelation.[1] There, John the apostle referred to Christ as the bridegroom.[2] Jesus,

---

[1] Rev 21:2, 9

[2] Jn 3:29

also, spoke of Himself that way, in reference to His pending death and His second coming.[3]

We've maybe heard of these analogies and accepted them, but at the same time, we have largely missed an important element – **PASSION**. The bride's for the bridegroom, the bridegroom's for His bride. How He yearns for her. How she loses herself in Him.

King Solomon sang of passion in his poetic song.

"Fasten me upon your heart as a seal of fire forevermore. This living, consuming flame will seal you as my prisoner of love. MY PASSION IS STRONGER than the chains of death and the grave, ALL CONSUMING as the very flashes of fire from the burning heart of God. Place this fierce, unrelenting fire over your entire being." (Song of Solomon 8:6 TPT)

This should be a picture of the church. We should be CONSUMED with the bridegroom, our PASSION for His Word burning in our hearts. We can't wait to speak of Him. We yearn to spend time with Him. He is our next breath, our greatest love.

Like a bride, adorned for her wedding day, that wonderful union of souls, we've prepared ourselves for His coming. We're the MATURE CHURCH, *"glorious and radiant, beautiful and holy, without fault or flaw."* His tenderness for us has made us that way.[4]

He should be our greatest desire, but instead, we are lethargic, slothful. We've allowed weeds to grow in the sanctuary. We've become apathetic to the move of the Spirit, with excuses why "God won't" and "We can't." We

---

[3] Mt 25:6; Mk 2:19

[4] Eph 5:28-30 TPT

are PASSIVE. We give no reaction to Him and inactive in the things of God.[5]

"I went by the field OF THE SLOTHFUL, and by the vineyard of the man void of understanding; And, lo, it was all grown over with thorns, and nettles had covered the face thereof, and the stone wall thereof was broken down. Then I saw, and considered it well: I looked upon it, and received instruction. Yet a little sleep, a little slumber, a little folding of the hands to sleep: So shall thy poverty come as one that travelleth; and thy want as an armed man." (Proverbs 24:30-34)

What a tremendous passage. It calls to mind the parable of the sower. In it, Jesus cautioned about becoming distracted. He said the cares of this life are like thorns in the garden, and they will prevent us from full reproduction and growth.[6] Instead of being CONSUMED with PASSION for the LIFE of God in us, we are indolent.[7]

Here is the truth—We tend to wait for God to give us an abundant harvest without making any effort to tend the garden.[8] We say, "This is just how I am," and expect God to move and hand the harvest to us.

No! We are responsible for the quality of the soil! We choose to become good soil, rich and fruitful, or to bury our seed amidst the rocks and the thorns.[9]

We are the five virgins who didn't bother to buy any oil, then the bridegroom came, and we missed the

---

[5] "Passive," Dictionary.com

[6] Lk 8:14

[7] H6102

[8] Lk 8:15

[9] Mk 4:14-20

celebration.[10] We weren't PASSIONATE. We weren't EAGER. And now cold to the Holy Spirit's presence, we've allowed error to creep in. We've accepted wrong doctrine and become content to coddle sin.[11]

Jude urged the church to action.

"Beloved, when I gave all diligence to write unto you of the common salvation, it was needful for me to write unto you, and exhort you that ye should EARNESTLY CONTEND for the faith which was once delivered unto the saints." (Jude 1:3)

Earnestly contend! Don't stop contending. Don't sit down and let go of what you've gained but take a stand of faith and KEEP STANDING.[12]

"I will therefore put you in remembrance," he continues.[13] Remember Egypt. Remember the consequences of Israel's sin. Then remember what you've been taught and build up yourselves so that lives will not be lost.

"But ye, beloved, BUILDING UP YOURSELVES on your most holy faith, praying in the Holy Ghost, Keep yourselves in the love of God, looking for the mercy of our Lord Jesus Christ unto eternal life. And of some have compassion, making a difference: And others save with fear, pulling them out of the fire; hating even the garment spotted by the flesh." (Jude 1:20-23)

God has given us, His church, all we need to QUENCH

---

[10] Mt 25:2-3
[11] Jud 1:4
[12] Eph 6:13-14
[13] Jud 1:5

the enemy's darts,[14] but instead of holding our shield up, we sit on it. It's become a bench, slowing sliding toward a dangerous cliff, dragging the weak and helpless, the lost along with us.

We are AFRAID to fight.

Timothy, the apostle Paul's son in the faith, faced great fear. Paul had been imprisoned for their beliefs, and it seemed Timothy struggled with this. Seeing his hesitation, Paul wrote him a moving letter and told him to STIR HIMSELF UP. He, too, urged remembrance.

"Remember the faith of your mother and grandmother," he said. "Remember what I've taught you. Remember how I laid hands on you and God called you. Refuse to be afraid or ashamed because it is not God's way. He is love and POWER and peace in your mind."[15]

We must consider these words, shake off our sleepiness, and STIR OURSELVES UP. We must become PASSIONATE for the bridegroom, anticipating His return.

We can't wait to see Him. We can't stop talking about Him. We've dressed in our best to please Him. We are thirsty for His voice, ardent. Because He's coming in clouds of glory, and an enthusiastic, anticipatory bride must make sure the whole world knows it.[16]

The People are the Church

God turned Abraham's gaze toward the sky and promised him a multitude of descendants. Then He gave him a vision of the seashore, and his children as more abundant than the sand. A divine promise, a covenant made with an old man and his wife, both past childbearing age,

---

[14] Eph 6:16
[15] 2Ti 1:5-7
[16] Mk 13:26

that would spread further than they could imagine.[17] Their descendants would become a mighty nation, whose God was known for His incredible acts.

"If my people, which are called by my name ..." (2 Chronicles 7:14)

"My people," God said again and again.

The phrase "my people" is used 231 times in the King James Bible and, until the prophecy of Zechariah, solely to mean Israel. Zechariah said, *"And MANY NATIONS shall be joined to the LORD in that day, and shall be MY PEOPLE."*[18]

Nations. A strange word in the ears of the Jews, which would not be fulfilled until one afternoon, almost 600 years later, when a man named Peter had a dream about dining on beasts considered unclean. Peter's dream would graft the Gentiles into the growing Christian church. Suddenly, the promise of the Holy Spirit, which fell at Pentecost, was available to anyone of any culture and any language, and belief in Jesus Christ, the Anointed One, spreading like wildfire.[19]

I find it amusing that Peter, who had denied Jesus three times in public, became such a loud voice for Christianity.[20] But God knows the heart, and He'd said, *"Upon this rock I will build my church; and the gates of hell shall not prevail against it."*[21]

Upon what rock? In a personal sense, upon Peter, whose name means "rock." I believe this was encouragement to him, who had doubted Christ so

---

[17] Heb 11:12
[18] Zec 2:11
[19] Act 10:11-15
[20] Mk 14:72
[21] Mt 16:18

completely.[22] But more specifically, Jesus referred to Peter's answer to His question in verses 15-16.

Jesus asked, *"But whom say ye that I am?"*

"And Simon Peter answered and said, Thou art THE CHRIST, the Son of the living God."

The foundation of the church and all that we would become is Jesus as THE CHRIST.

The word "Christ" in the original Greek means "the anointed."[23]

Anointing with oil was done over kings and priests to dedicate them for their divine office. It was done during prayer for healing.[24] It is used throughout the Word of God to mean the presence of God, or the Holy Spirit, working through and in someone.

The anointing is the POWER of God that saves, heals, and delivers.

Peter, in that moment of PASSION, standing face-to-face with Cornelius, a Roman man seeking an experience with the Jewish God ... Peter, filled with the Holy Spirit and aware of the dream he'd been given, makes a statement about Jesus' life and ministry that is the basis of all the church would become.

"How God ANOINTED Jesus of Nazareth with the Holy Ghost and with POWER: who went about DOING GOOD, and HEALING all that were OPPRESSED OF THE DEVIL; for GOD WAS WITH HIM." (Acts 10:38)

Here is what the Anointed One did, why He did it,

---

[22] Jn 21:15

[23] G5547

[24] Mk 6:13; Jas 5:14

how He did it, and the end result. The four gospels, Matthew, Mark, Luke, and John, give the details of what Jesus' said and who He touched, as well as the important story of His crucifixion, but Peter's statement gives much needed revelation and insight.

"How God anointed."

God set Jesus apart for His divine office. It was God's will that He came to fulfill the Mosaic law and provide the sacrifice needed to obtain our redemption.[25] This is important to understand.

But also, we must know that God anointed Jesus with POWER to DO GOOD and HEAL those OPPRESSED OF THE DEVIL. That was His purpose, what He spoke and what He did.

The people of that day were astonished at His preaching, *how* He spoke as well as the miracles that followed, when God's healing touch was not unusual in their history at all.[26]

The Bible is a book of miracles, extraordinary signs and wonders done by the power of God that are unexplainable in any other way except to say they were God's supernatural desire. From the first chapter of Genesis, where God performs surgery on Adam without pain or time needed for healing, to the birth of Isaac from a woman too old to naturally conceive, and also, the extraordinary healing of Naaman, captain of the host of the king of Syria, of an incurable skin disease, God proved His desire to heal time and time again.[27]

Moses at God's instruction held up a bronze pole

---

[25] Mt 5:17

[26] Mt 22:33; Mk 6:2; Mk 7:37

[27] Ge 2:21; Ge 21:3; 2Ki 5:14

with a fiery serpent carved on its tip and said anyone who'd look upon it wouldn't die of snakebite but would live.[28] King Hezekiah was at the point of death and pleaded for his life. The prophet Isaiah came to him and said God heard his prayer and had granted him 15 more years.[29] Job had lost everything, including his health, and had spoken untruths about God. God set him straight in a powerful passage of Scripture, and when Job repented of his sins, God blessed him with twice as much as before.[30]

These are but a few examples, and they should have been known to those who witnessed His miracles, especially those trained in the Synagogue. Instead, John 1:10-11 says, *"He was in the world, and the world was made by him, and the world knew him not. He came unto his own, and his own received him not."*

This verse points to Jesus' divinity, stated earlier in verses 1-4. There, He's called the Word of God, the Life of God, and the Light of creation.

In Colossians 1:16-17 we can confirm this. It states, *"For by him were all things created, that are in heaven, and that are in earth, visible and invisible, whether they be thrones, or dominions, or principalities, or powers: all things were created by him, and for him: And he is before all things, and by him all things consist."*

Now, add in Jesus' statement, recorded in John 8:58: *"Verily, verily, I say unto you, Before Abraham was, I am."*

A reference to the words of God spoken to Moses[31] and a remark that made people very angry. How dare He equate Himself equal with God?

This fully shows their ignorance of what had been

---

[28] Num 21:8

[29] 2Ki 20:4

[30] Job 42:10, 12

[31] Ex 3:14

prophesied throughout history.

Isaiah had drawn a complete portrait of Jesus' life and death. He included physical and mental healing in it, as well as the rebirth of the spirit of man.

"Yet he was the one who carried OUR SICKNESSES and endured the torment OF OUR SUFFERINGS. We viewed him as one who was being punished for something he himself had done, as one who was struck down by God and brought low. But it was because of our rebellious deeds that he was pierced and because of our sins that he was crushed. He endured the punishment that made us COMPLETELY WHOLE, and in his wounding WE FOUND OUR HEALING." (Isaiah 53:4-5 TPT)

The King James Version reads, *"Surely he hath borne our griefs, and carried our sorrows."*[32]

"Griefs" in the original Hebrew means "malady, anxiety, calamity, disease, grief."[33] "Sorrows" means "anguish, affliction, pain, sorrow."[34]

All the anxiety and anguish we would ever have, all of our heartache, disease, and physical pains, all of our sins were placed on Jesus Christ.

Though Jesus was fully God, He set His divine nature aside to live as a man, though without committing sin.[35] He didn't heal those OPPRESSED OF THE DEVIL through His own power but through the ANOINTING and POWER of the Holy Ghost.

---

[32] Is 53:4

[33] H2483

[34] H4341

[35] 2Co 5:21

Dunamis

The word "power" used in Acts 10:38 is the Greek word "dunamis."[36] It is also translated *"mighty works," "wonderful works," "mighty deeds," "miracles," "strength,"* and *"virtue."*

Strong's Exhaustive Concordance of Old and New Testament Words defines it as "force" or specifically "miraculous power."

Thayer's Greek Definitions expands on this to include: "inherent power, power residing in a thing by virtue of its nature, or which a person or thing exerts and puts forth; moral power and excellence of soul; the power and influence which belong to riches and wealth; power and resources arising from numbers; power consisting in or resting upon armies, forces, hosts."

This puts Peter's words in an incredible light.

"How God anointed Jesus of Nazareth with the Holy Ghost and with ***DUNAMIS****: who went about DOING GOOD, and HEALING all that were OPPRESSED OF THE DEVIL; for GOD WAS WITH HIM."* (Acts 10:38)

The inherent power of God, the power OF HIS NATURE, the power HE EXERTS, God's MORAL POWER AND EXCELLENCE OF SOUL, His INFLUENCE and the power of His RICHES, all of His RESOURCES combined, did good and healed those oppressed of the devil.

These are the same statements Jesus made. In John 5, three times, He said He'd come to do the Father's will. He only did what He saw the Father do. The LIFE in Him was the Father's.[37] Three equal statements with important meaning.

---

[36] G1411

[37] Jn 5:19, 26, 30

Jesus came to do the Father's will, and it was the Father's will to DO GOOD and HEAL those OPPRESSED OF THE DEVIL. The LIFE in Him that DID GOOD and HEALED was the LIFE of the Father.

We must know this to fully, PASSIONATELY, become the church. In this is complete salvation. We've read John 3:16, *"For God SO LOVED the world that he gave his only begotten Son, that whosoever believeth in him should not perish, but have everlasting life,"* and have stopped there.

Keep reading into verse 17.

"For God sent not his Son into the world to condemn the world; but that the world through him MIGHT BE SAVED."

The word *"saved"* is the Greek word "sozo" meaning to "save, deliver, protect, heal, preserve, make whole."[38]

Notice, how exhaustive it is.

God's love for the sinful world was SO GREAT in size AND in quality. He loved man despite their sins. He is that merciful. But He also loved them SO MUCH that His salvation is of the finest, most complete, type. Everything men and women would ever need is included in it.

This is no dime store purchase, but one made in blood.

Jesus came to spread the GOOD NEWS that we are free from the devil's oppression in every area of our lives – spiritually, mentally, and physically.[39] Not to give a motivational talk, but to demonstrate the DUNAMIS of God, to show a forgetful, ignorant people the NATURE OF GOD, His EXCELLENCE OF SOUL, His mighty INFLUENCE.

---

[38] G4982

[39] "Gospel," Mk 1:1

Jesus came to display the incredible glory of God to weak, human vessels.

"You don't have to die in your sins. You don't have to live lame or blind. You can be free from leprosy. The adultery you indulged in, go and sin no more."

He said all of these things without condemnation but, instead, with God's undeserved grace. He was gentle and compassionate. This was the heavenly Father's will.[40]

But, oh, how the church has forgotten it and turned the GOSPEL of CHRIST into something smaller, weaker, and less powerful.

Scripture fulfilled

Jesus went home to Nazareth, and as He did every place He went, He entered the synagogue to read the Scriptures. He chose a passage in Isaiah then, when He'd finished reading, made a statement that startled everyone.

"And when he had opened the book, he found the place where it was written, The SPIRIT OF THE LORD is upon me, because he hath ANOINTED me to preach THE GOSPEL to the poor; he hath sent me TO HEAL the brokenhearted, to PREACH DELIVERANCE to the captives, and RECOVERING OF SIGHT to the blind, to SET AT LIBERTY them that are bruised, To preach the acceptable year of the Lord. And he closed the book, and he gave it again to the minister, and sat down. And the eyes of all them that were in the synagogue were fastened on him. And he began to say unto them, This day is this scripture fulfilled in your ears." (Luke 4:17-21)

It says, the people wondered at His words. They heard the heart of God speaking to them; they heard God's

[40] Mt 11:29 VOICE; Mt 20:34; Mk 1:41; Mk 8:2

grace yet questioned why Jesus would apply those verses to Himself.

"Isn't this Joseph's son?" they asked.[41]

Jesus had some pointed words for them, right then.

"No prophet is accepted in his own country," He said.[42]

His calling Himself a prophet and His calling them out on their doubtful behavior set them off. The crowd grew so angry they tried to push Him over the hilltop to His death.[43] Instead of believing such GOOD NEWS – here stood the long-awaited fulfillment of Scripture – these people who had been IN THE TEMPLE for worship reacted in anger, murder, and dissent.

We must see in them a troubling picture of ourselves and commit ourselves afresh to the words Jesus spoke. First, that He was ANOINTED to preach the GOOD NEWS.

The word "anointed" used here, *chriō,* means consecrated, or dedicated.

To be consecrated is to be set apart as sacred.[44] Jesus was consecrated to the Father's will. The Holy Spirit was upon Him because the WILL OF GOD through Him was to HEAL, to DELIVER, to RECOVER, and to SET AT LIBERTY. The NATURE OF GOD, all that God is, HIS EXCELLENCE, or we could say, His HONOR, and His INFLUENCE, as well as His MIGHT had come to earth to bring HEALING and FREEDOM.

These truths are repeated throughout the gospels. Matthew 4:23-24 in the Voice Translation says:

"And so Jesus went throughout Galilee. He taught in the synagogues. He preached the GOOD NEWS of the

---

[41] Lk 4:22
[42] Lk 4:24
[43] Lk 4:29
[44] G5548

Kingdom, and He HEALED people, RIDDING THEIR BODIES OF SICKNESS AND DISEASE. Word spread all over Syria, as more and more sick people came to Him. The innumerable ill who came before Him had all sorts of diseases, they were in crippling pain; they were possessed by demons; they had seizures; they were paralyzed. BUT JESUS HEALED THEM ALL."

Not a few or a handful of people were healed, but everyone, the crippled, the demon possessed. EVERYONE.

In Matthew 9:35, we read this again.

"Jesus went through many towns and villages. He taught in their synagogues. He preached the good news of the kingdom of God. HE HEALED EVERY DISEASE AND SICKNESS." (VOICE)

Every sickness. Every disease. There are many more equal statements in God's Word.

Matthew 14:14 says, *"Though Jesus wanted solitude [to mourn John's death], when He saw the crowds, He had compassion on them, and HE HEALED the sick and the lame."*[45]

Jesus turned aside from His grief, His compassion for the sick overwhelming Him.

Read also Matthew 15:30: *"Crowds thronged to Him there, bringing the lame, the maimed, the blind, the crippled, the mute, and many other sick and broken people. They laid them at His feet, AND HE HEALED THEM."*[46]

Now, turn over to the gospel of Mark. In Mark 3:10-11, it says, *"For HE HAD HEALED MANY; insomuch that they*

---

[45] VOICE

[46] VOICE

pressed upon him for to touch him, as many as had plagues. And unclean spirits, when they saw him, fell down before him, and cried, saying, Thou art the Son of God."

It's interesting to note that demonic spirits knew Him as the Son of God. In more than one instance, the people didn't believe, but the demons testified of who He was.[47]

Why? Not simply because of who He was as God, but because THE ANOINTING flowed in Him. Because the power of God had come to HEAL, to SAVE and DELIVER, and they were power*less* in the face of it.

Luke 6:19 says, *"And the whole multitude sought to touch him: for there went VIRTUE out of him, and healed them all."* The word *"virtue"* here is DUNAMIS again. The power of GOD'S NATURE flowed from Him and healing came.

This was God's will, remember? **Jesus did the Father's will.** Jehovah who healed in Old Testament times desired to heal through Jesus.

Jesus was sent to earth as Emmanuel, God with us.[48] Then also, He said in John 10:30, *"I and my Father are one."* As "one" with the Father, as "God with us" in the flesh, Jesus did what the Father wanted done – He healed all who were sick, diseased, and tormented.

We can find yet one more proof of Jesus' calling in the angel's words to Mary.

*"And the angel answered and said unto her, The HOLY GHOST SHALL COME UPON THEE, and the POWER [**DUNAMIS**] of the Highest shall overshadow thee: therefore also that holy thing which shall be born of thee shall be called THE SON OF GOD. And, behold, thy cousin Elisabeth,*

---

[47] Mt 8:29; Lk 4:41
[48] Mt 1:23

she hath also conceived a son in her old age: and this is the sixth month with her, who was called barren. FOR WITH GOD NOTHING SHALL BE IMPOSSIBLE." (Luke 1:35-37)

Notice, in Luke's account, conception is not mentioned, nor her virginity. Instead, it was that the DUNAMIS, the power of GOD'S NATURE, His MIGHT, would place in her a holy child. Through the Holy Spirit's POWER, she conceived the SON OF GOD.

The Holy Spirit's work to create what should not happen by natural law is the focus. The ANOINTING on her is what we needed to know about.

Vincent's Word Studies gives even more force to the angel's words, further defining the last verse, *"For with God nothing shall be impossible."* This is a magnificent thought on its own, but according to scholars, it should read: *"Every (πᾶν) word of God SHALL NOT (οὐκ) BE POWERLESS."*

Isn't that incredible?

Every word of God is POWERFUL. No words are POWERLESS, and the POWER of those words HEALED, soothed broken hearts, had compassion on the sick, and delivered from the OPPRESSION OF THE DEVIL.

Or we could say, the OPPRESSION OF THE DEVIL kept people sick, brokenhearted, lame, blind, and demon possessed. Jesus came to DESTROY all of that.

These are the words of 1 John 3:8.

"FOR THIS PURPOSE the Son of God was manifested, that he might DESTROY THE WORKS OF THE DEVIL."

That is why Jesus came. He came to DESTROY what the devil had done to people in every area of their lives. It really is that simple. That awesome.

Chapter 2

The Triumphant Church

A man or woman who has experienced an event cannot be told it has not happened. Some 3.5 million Jews survived the Holocaust. Of those, Between 250,000 and 300,000 survived death marches and concentration camps. You cannot convince them it didn't happen because they were there. They experienced it.[1]

Similarly, those who were not there, who have no eyewitness knowledge, cannot possibly fully understand what it was like to survive something so horrible.

On a more day-to-day front, a man who cannot swim does not know what it is like to be able to swim. He cannot tell you how to swim. He hasn't done it before. He isn't aware of the feel of the water while swimming. Until he takes lessons and learns, he will not be free in the area of swimming.

Another example: I love those videos that go around the internet where some person who is colorblind receives their first pair of corrective vision glasses. Suddenly, their world of brown and gray becomes vibrant red, green, purple, and yellow. There's an important lesson in that because the world was all those colors all along. They simply couldn't see it.

I grew up hearing how God healed today. I even attended meetings where healing was preached, but being frank, it had never happened to me, so I didn't understand it like someone who'd had cancer, who'd faced the fact they might die, then God had healed them completely. It's one

---

[1] https://en.wikipedia.org/wiki/Holocaust_survivors#Numbers_of_survivors

thing to say you believe in healing and another to live it by faith.

1 John 3:8 says Jesus came to DESTROY THE WORKS OF THE DEVIL. Vincent's Word Studies defines the phrase "might destroy" and includes a powerful quote:

"Lit., *dissolve, loosen*. 'The works of the devil are represented as having a certain consistency and coherence. They show a kind of solid front. But Christ, by His coming, has revealed them in their complete unsubstantiality. He has 'undone' the seeming bonds by which they were held together.'" (Westcott)."

This is so marvelous! **Jesus Christ, the Anointed One, through His death and Resurrection, dissolved the devil's works.** What "works?" The grip of sin and sickness in man. Oppression that caused people to live in pain and mental anguish. Jesus showed the devil's works of disease and injury as being unsubstantial.

Something "unsubstantial" has "no foundation in fact." It is "without material substance" or, we could say, it is "flimsy."[2]

How great this revelation is!

The devil is the deceiver, the father of lies, and the oppression of man. All of these depictions are given in the Word of God.[3] The devil works to keep men and women in bondage to sickness and disease, to anxiety and depression, to poverty and lack. Where Jesus came to set people free, to shine the light of the Word of Truth in their hearts, the devil works with all that is in him to convince people that we must live bound by sin, sickness, and lack.

---

[2] Dictionary.com

[3] Jn 8:44; Rev 12:9; Act 10:38

Teacher and Bible scholar Rick Renner says that the word "devil" is not a name but a job description. How much the church needs that knowledge. The devil will use anything he can to destroy people. He'll use religion, which often says the power of God was for yesterday. You won't find this in any Scripture. He uses carnality. If he can keep people thinking about their troubles, keep them defending their ungodly behaviors, then he retains the upper hand.

He uses strife. He keeps us arguing with each other over trivial things when the Word of God says strife brings *"confusion and every evil work."*[4] How serious that is. If we open the door to strife, we let in everything else the devil wants to do.

But there is GOOD NEWS! **Jesus HAS DESTROYED the devil's works. He has made him unsubstantial.** That was Jesus' purpose, and anything that says differently is going against the Scriptures. For from Genesis to Revelation, God has not changed. His heart for every man and woman who has ever lived was joy and blessing.

Malachi 3:6 states, *"For I am the LORD, I change not."*

As He was thousands of years ago, He still is today.

Hebrews 13:8 puts a period on the end of the thought. *"Jesus Christ the same yesterday, and to day, and for ever."*

He is Jesus, the ANOINTED ONE, sent to HEAL; He's the God of POWER yesterday, but also today, in the present, and forever into the future. He's THE SAME God of POWER He always has been. And on THIS ROCK, the rock of CHRIST'S ANOINTING to HEAL and SET FREE, He will build the church, *"and the gates of hell shall not prevail against it."*[5]

---

[4] Jas 3:16
[5] Mt 16:18

The Passion Translation makes this verse very clear: *"I give you the name Peter, a stone. AND THIS TRUTH OF WHO I AM will be the bedrock foundation on which I will build my church—my legislative assembly, and the power of death will not be able to overpower it!"*

How great is that? I also like the VOICE translation's rendering of the final phrase: *"The church will reign triumphant even at the gates of hell."*

This is a truth the church needs to grasp, both individually and corporately. The church isn't a building. It's the people, and **the people are the body of Christ united to be TRIUMPHANT over hell and the works of hell.** The power of death cannot overpower the PASSIONATE CHURCH.

Instead, God's children are to do what Jesus did. We see this truth in Ephesians.

"And [God] hath put all things UNDER HIS [CHRIST'S] FEET, and gave him to be the head over all things to the church, Which is his body, the FULNESS OF HIM THAT FILLETH all in all." (Ephesians 1:22-23)

ALL THINGS are under the ANOINTED ONE'S feet. He is TRIUMPHANT over ALL THINGS.

He is the head of the church, meaning the people who make up the church., and the church is the FULNESS of THE ANOINTED ONE.

That word "fulness" means "completion" or said with more detail, it is "what fills (as contents, supplement, copiousness, multitude), or (objectively) what is filled (as container, performance, period)."[6]

How much I love that!

---

[6] G4138

We, the church, are both what is filled *and* what fills us—THE ANOINTING.

How marvelous! Jesus came to DO GOOD and HEAL through the DUNAMIS of the Holy Spirit. Jesus also came to FILL US so that we can work DUNAMIS on the earth.

He didn't say, "This is what will happen while I'm here and then 'good luck.'"

No, He equipped us *"for the work of the ministry."*[7]

We can see this in His words to His disciples. He anointed His disciples to go into the surrounding towns and PREACH the gospel and HEAL and drive out demons.

"Jesus called His twelve disciples to Him. He endowed them with THE AUTHORITY to heal sickness and disease and to drive demons out of those who were possessed." (Matthew 10:1 VOICE)

The King James Version uses the word "power" where this says "authority." This word in the Greek language is *exousia,* meaning "authority."[8] Several times, we are told Jesus spoke with such authority that the people around Him noticed.[9]

Here, He gives this same authority to His disciples but with a purpose – to HEAL and DRIVE OUT demons.

"And as ye go, PREACH, saying, The kingdom of heaven is at hand. HEAL the sick, CLEANSE the lepers, RAISE the dead, CAST OUT devils: freely ye have received, freely give." (Matthew 10:7-8 VOICE)

Note, the KINGDOM OF HEAVEN was the topic of the

---

[7] Eph 4:12

[8] G1849

[9] Mt 7:29; Mk 1:22; Lk 4:32, 36

sermon. "At hand" means it was present with them. It is also interesting to note that to "preach" means "to proclaim with a loud voice."[10]

They weren't to slip in and whisper it in a few ears, but walk the streets, shouting the GOOD NEWS, and healings were the results which would follow. God wanted to show His great love to the people, and that love healed and cleansed through the ANOINTING, which worked in the disciples' hands.[11]

Jesus wasn't physically with them. If you read His complete instructions. He tells them what to carry, how to act, and how to speak. They were sent with His AUTHORITY over the OPPRESSION OF THE DEVIL.

The account in Luke expands on this. Luke 10:1 says:

"After these things the Lord appointed other seventy also, and sent them two and two BEFORE his face into every city and place, whither he himself would come."

They went BEFORE Him where He WOULD COME, so He wasn't with them at the time, but they ministered in His stead. Then see His instructions:

"And HEAL THE SICK that are therein, and say unto them, The KINGDOM OF GOD IS COME NIGH unto you." (Luke 10:9)

Here it is again. The Kingdom of God was near, that being Jesus and the GOOD NEWS that HEALING had come. God's will was to HEAL through the disciples. They represented the Kingdom!

---

[10] Joseph Benson's Commentary on the Old and New Testaments
[11] Jn 3:16

How? Well, we must read further.

"And the seventy returned again with joy, saying, Lord, even the devils are subject unto us THROUGH THY NAME." (Luke 10:17)

It wasn't that the disciples were special because they were His disciples, but that the AUTHORITY OF HIS NAME sent the devils packing. Just as demons cried out that Jesus was the Son of God, recognizing His power and authority, they saw this authority and power in the disciples' hands as well. What Jesus did, they did IN HIS NAME.

The centurion who inquired for the healing of His servant remarked on this. He refused to allow Jesus to travel to his home, but said, *"SPEAK THE WORD ONLY, and my servant shall be healed. For I am a man UNDER AUTHORITY, having soldiers under me: and I say to this man, Go, and he goeth; and to another, Come, and he cometh; and to my servant, Do this, and he doeth it."*[12]

I've worked for my mother's ministry for over 20 years. I have the authority to do certain things in her name. She doesn't have to be there, but when I say I represent her, people listen. My speaking is like her speaking.

The centurion understood this. When Jesus spoke, God spoke.

Jesus replied that He hadn't seen faith of that size in all of Israel.[13] It took a Roman, a Gentile, to understand the AUTHORITY of Jesus' name.

The ANOINTING, working through the disciples, set people free FROM SATAN'S OPPRESSION. In Jesus' name, the Holy Spirit came to HEAL. Pay attention to Jesus' next

---

[12] Mt 8:8-9

[13] Mt 10:6; Mt 15:24

words from the story in Luke.

"I beheld Satan as lightning fall from heaven. Behold, I give unto you [AUTHORITY] to tread on serpents and scorpions, and over all the POWER OF THE ENEMY: and nothing shall by any means hurt you. Notwithstanding in this rejoice not, that the spirits are subject unto you; but rather rejoice, because your names are written in heaven." (Luke 10:18-20)

His first remark isn't, "Good job," but a comment about Satan's fall. This seems incongruous, at first. But then, He turns their attention to His AUTHORITY and what it will do over ALL that the enemy, Satan, tries to use to destroy people. He also speaks of their protection. NOTHING, Jesus says, shall hurt them. That's an incredible promise.

But then, the NAME OF JESUS is above every other name in the present world and in the future one.[14] God's AUTHORITY trumps the devil's from now until the end of time.

Greater Works

God's POWER and AUTHORITY are stronger than anything the devil has up his sleeve. We saw this in Jesus' instructions to His disciples. They went before Him, preaching the GOOD NEWS in a loud voice, and signs and wonders followed. They spoke Jesus' name, and the power of His name brought the Father's will of complete salvation into the lives of the people.

Jesus explained this, once more, in a conversation with His disciples. Phillip asked to see the Father, and Jesus was a little incredulous.

---

[14] Eph 1:21

"How can you keep asking to see the Father? Don't you believe Me when I say I abide in the Father and the Father dwells in Me? I'm not making this up as I go along. The Father has given Me these truths that I have been speaking to you, and HE EMPOWERS ALL MY ACTIONS. Accept these truths: I am in the Father, and the Father is in Me. If you have trouble believing based on My words, believe BECAUSE OF THE THINGS I HAVE DONE. I tell you the truth: whoever believes in Me will be able to do what I have done, BUT THEY WILL DO EVEN GREATER THINGS, because I will return to be with the Father. Whatever you ask for in My name, I will do it so that the Father will get glory from the Son. Let Me say it again: if you ask for anything in My name, I will do it." (John 14:9-14 VOICE)

"Look at those who are healed and delivered and set free," Jesus said. "This is the Father's will. 'He empowers all my actions.'"

I love that phrase. **God's POWER, His DUNAMIS, saved and healed and set free, and by that, we know Jesus' identity.** This should not be confusing to us. Watch Olympic Gold Medalist Dominic Dawes do her floor routine and there is no doubt in your mind she is a gymnast. Attend a concert with Andreas Bocelli and you know immediately he is a professional singer. Their works prove who they are.

Jesus works proved the Father's will to heal. To think of the devil as being behind demonic deliverance is ludicrous. Jesus made this clear in an exchange with the Pharisees. They accused Him of using the devil to drive out demons, and He said, *"And if Satan cast out Satan, he is divided against himself; how shall then his kingdom stand?"*[15]

[15] Mt 12:26

Think of any major corporation. Split it into factions and warring with each other, the company will collapse. Unity is necessary to success in business. This is true in the spirit realm as well.

Jesus went on to point out that the Mosaic law provided prayer for healing, so if they thought He was doing Satan's work, then the same could be said of them.[16]

Hear, again, Jesus' words to these men who would become THE CHURCH.

"Verily, verily, I say unto you, He that believeth on me, THE WORKS THAT I DO SHALL HE DO ALSO; and GREATER WORKS THAN THESE SHALL HE DO; because I go unto my Father." (John 14:12)

The CHURCH is sent out to do GREATER WORKS. That's not a quality promise, not *better* works. It's a QUANTITY promise. One soldier can only fight so many of the enemy at once, and then, in only one location at a time. But when Jesus sent the seventy out, now look at how much can be done, and after His Resurrection, watch the church grow and expand and see how many lives were changed. Thousands!

The church is meant to do GREATER WORKS. We are to continue Jesus' ministry of HEALING and DELIVERANCE, and Jesus gave us the tools to do it. We have the AUTHORITY of His name and the Holy Spirit's ANOINTING, DUNAMIS. Whatever we ask in faith, it is like Jesus is asking.

We read this in Jesus' words in Mark 16.

"And THESE SIGNS shall follow them that believe; IN MY NAME shall they cast out devils; they shall speak with

---

[16] Mt 12:24-28

new tongues; They shall take up serpents; and if they drink any deadly thing, it shall not hurt them; they shall lay hands on the sick, and they SHALL RECOVER." (Mark 16:17-18)

These signs SHALL FOLLOW. They SHALL RECOVER. These are unquestionable. It SHALL HAPPEN to those who believe, to those who ask in the authority of Jesus' name.

We, the church, are Jesus' representatives on the earth. We are a light that people can turn to and be set free of the devil's destruction.

Jesus said, *"Healthy people don't need a doctor—sick people do. I have come to call not those who think they are righteous, but those who know they are sinners."*[17]

The church should be where those who need help can find help. Not simply a gathering of sanctimonious people, reminding themselves how sanctimonious they are. That smacks of arrogance and pride, which God is against 100%.

But instead, the church is a place where the ANOINTING flows. It is where imperfect people come in contact with a perfect God and come away changed.

That is why Jesus came to earth and lived as a man and died a cruel death. God would draw all men back to Him,[18] and there, in His presence, ALL of our needs are met.[19] Spirit, soul, AND body.[20]

This is God's heart. His greatest desire is for our complete healing.

And know this, God will never do anything halfway. He cannot save the spirit of man while neglecting the soul

[17] Mk 2:17 NLT

[18] Jn 12:32

[19] Jn 15:10

[20] 1Th 5:23; Heb 4:12

and the body. He's an ALL THINGS God.[21]

He's proven this time and time again.

All Things

We expect everything in our lives of faith to be dramatic. We're on a constant uphill struggle, an endless battle, slashing at the enemy on every side. We must cross rivers and climb mountains, our lives in constant peril.

There's some truth to that imagery, of course. But our days are full of much smaller moments, everyday decisions that require wisdom and understanding to perform. Look at Philippians 4:13: *"I can do ALL THINGS through Christ which strengtheneth me."* That includes seemingly silly tasks as well.

"But the Comforter, which is the Holy Ghost, whom the Father will send in my name, he shall teach you ALL THINGS, and bring ALL THINGS to your remembrance, whatsoever I have said unto you." (John 14:26)

We're afraid to pray for those. But I can do all things because the Holy Spirit shall teach me all things. That's profound. And comforting.

When some new responsibility falls on my desk, even if I feel like I'm not smart enough, I know the One who is. This could be as simple as doing your taxes. Or maybe your teenage son or daughter needs help finding "x" on their algebra assignment. Maybe you promised to take a friend somewhere you aren't sure you can find, GPS or not. Those are also "all things".

"And God is able to make ALL grace abound

---

[21] Mk 10:27; 2Co 5:17; 2Co 9:8

toward you; that ye, ALWAYS having ALL SUFFICIENCY in ALL THINGS, may abound to EVERY good work." (2 Corinthians 9:8)

To "abound" is "to exceed a fixed number of measure."[22] It's to have more than you need. All grace. All sufficiency. ALL THINGS.

God cares about every part of our lives, no matter how trivial they may seem. He wants us to "abound" when we bake a cake for our mom's birthday, when we call the cable company to straighten out our bill, when we take our car to be serviced and need to choose the right auto repair shop.

Sometimes it's the small things that cripple us the most. We don our armor to fight giants but take it off when it's Uncle John asking for help to clear trees. Or to locate a baby gift for our cousin's wife, who we don't particularly get along with. Or the refrigerator needs replacing, but we have no idea what to buy.

I want to be sufficient in those tasks, too. Sufficient means "adequate to the purpose."[23] God is more than adequate!

I've found, in my life, personally, that my need to shift responsibility onto others – a "you do it for me" attitude – never works out. Any time I think I can get him or her to take care of it, it'll fall even harder on my shoulders, and those moments are when I pray, "I can do this through Christ."

I need supernatural strength to walk the dog some days, especially when it's cold and windy and she's decided to play.

---

[22] Thayer's Greek Definitions

[23] Dictionary.com

I can do all things and have patience. I can do all things and understand how to fill out this form. I can do all things and find a perfect vacation rental within my budget. I can do all things and select the right doctor, hair salon, or lawn company.

All things includes ALL things.

"And the Lord give thee understanding in ALL THINGS." (2 Timothy 1:7)

Does a God who knows our soul, who saw us when we were made in secret, a God of such infinite detail to create the smallest part of us, abandon us when we need to change a flat tire? He's only here for me when I'm slugging it out in some spiritual battle, but not when I've had an argument with my spouse?[24]

No, that's when I need understanding the most.

"What shall we then say to these things? If God be for us, who can be against us? He that spared not his own Son, but delivered him up for us all, how shall he not with him also freely give us ALL THINGS?" (Romans 8:31-32)

I know God is for me; therefore, who can be against me? Always. For everything. Even if today it's as small as calling the electric company. God is with me for that, too. We've lost sight of this, like Peter troubled by our fears of the world around us.

After Jesus prophesied Peter would deny Him three times,[25] He gave His disciples moving words of comfort.

---

[24] Ps 139:14-16
[25] Jn 13:36

"Don't worry or surrender to your fear. For you've believed in God, now trust and believe in me also. My Father's house has many dwelling places. If it were otherwise, I would tell you plainly, because I go to prepare a place for you to rest. (John 14:1-2 TPT)

Our fears of any type mean we do not believe in God's promise to supply ALL THINGS. It means we think He won't come through. He won't be SUFFICIENT. He won't do ENOUGH. He will hold back on His MIGHT, His POWER TO HEAL and to SAVE.

But Jesus bids us to TRUST.

"If ye love me, keep my commandments. And I will pray the Father, and he shall give you ANOTHER COMFORTER, that he may abide with you for ever; Even THE SPIRIT OF TRUTH; whom the world cannot receive, because it seeth him not, neither knoweth him: but ye know him; FOR HE DWELLETH WITH YOU, AND SHALL BE IN YOU. I will not leave you comfortless: I WILL COME TO YOU." (John 14:15-18)

Do not miss the structure of Jesus' words. First, He's speaking to the disciples, to the CHURCH. Then, He refers to the Holy Spirit as the COMFORTER and the Spirit of TRUTH.

The word "comforter" is more properly rendered "advocate," meaning one who intercedes for you in court. It can also be "monitor, teacher, or helper."[26] It is used three times of the Holy Spirit and one time of the Lord Jesus.[27]

We see this in the above passage. Jesus says, "You know *him*," and "*He* dwells with you." Then He follows it

---

[26] G3875; Albert Barnes' Notes on the Bible

[27] Jn 14:26; Jn 15:26; Jn 16:7; 1Jn 2:1

with, *"I will not leave you comfortless. I will come to you,"* speaking of Himself.

You will not have Jesus Christ without the Holy Spirit, and you cannot have the Holy Spirit without Christ. The Holy Spirit is our Comforter, and Jesus promised He would not leave us without comfort. These truths work together, and they create our TRUST in God.

I like how Albert Barnes' Notes on the Bible outlines the Holy Spirit's purpose as stated in John 14:16. It says, He is:

"1. To comfort the disciples; to be with them in his [Jesus'] absence and to supply his place; and this is properly expressed by the word Comforter. 2. To teach them, or remind them of truth; and this might be expressed by the word monitor or teacher, Joh_14:26; Joh_15:26-27. 3. To aid them in their work; to advocate their cause, or to assist them in advocating the cause of religion in the world, and in bringing sinners to repentance; and this may be expressed by the word advocate, Joh_16:7-13. It was also by the Spirit that they were enabled to stand before kings and magistrates, and boldly to speak in the name of Jesus, Mat_10:20."

This sounds like ALL THINGS. Doesn't it? The Holy Spirit brings *personal* comfort, filling us with Christ and teaching us from God's Word so we may walk wisely in our daily life, and the Holy Spirit brings comfort to the church, so that we speak boldly in Jesus' name, as WITNESSES.

We are the PASSIONATE CHURCH because the Holy Spirit works in us and through us, because He is upon us. We are FEARLESS in the face of evil and unbelief through God's POWER in us. We KNOW TRUTH because the Holy Spirit guides us, and we cannot be silenced.

I don't know about you, but that's incredible to me. I never need to be INSUFFICIENT because the Holy Spirit is my Comforter FOREVER. He is certain. He can be relied upon.

The commentary says this so wonderfully.

"Not that he [The Holy Spirit] should remain with you for a few years, as I [Jesus] have done, and then leave you, but be with you in all places to the close of your life. He shall be your constant guide and attendant."

The Holy Spirit is our constant guide and attendant. How much I love that!

He is ALL THINGS. He is the POWER that enables us to stand, bold in faith. He is the MANIFESTATION of Jesus in us. He is all these things FOREVER. What Jesus was on earth, the works that He did, GREATER WORKS will believers do because THE HOLY SPIRIT CAME.

He will not let us forget Jesus is Christ, the Anointed One. He will remind us of the TRUTH.

Now let's add in a thought recorded in John 15.

"But when the Comforter is come, whom I [Jesus] will send unto you from the Father, even the Spirit of truth, which proceedeth from the Father, HE SHALL TESTIFY OF ME: And YE ALSO shall BEAR WITNESS, because ye have been with me from the beginning." (John 15:26-27)

Jesus sent the Holy Spirit because the Father desired it. He only did what He saw the Father do, right? We read that earlier.

Therefore, the power of God, His DUNAMIS to do ALL THINGS, is the Father's will for me, for you, and for the church. Through the Holy Spirit, we offer comfort; we have FAITH. In the Holy Spirit's power, the EXCELLENCE of God, we do GREATER WORKS that "bear witness" of Him.

To "bear witness" is to "testify, give evidence, bear record, give honest report, give testimony."[28] It means you know something 100% and can state it truthfully.

Well, what did Jesus' disciples know? What were they to testify of?

"How God anointed Jesus of Nazareth with the Holy Ghost and with power: who went about doing good, and healing all that were oppressed of the devil; for God was with him." (Acts 10:38)

That was the testimony! That Jesus through the power of the Holy Spirit did GOOD and that good HEALED those OPPRESSED OF THE DEVIL because GOD WAS WITH HIM.

The WORKS are the WITNESS! They TESTIFY of Him.

Jesus' disciples were to GO and DO like Him. He would ascend to the Father, but the Holy Spirit would FILL them and ENABLE them to do ALL THINGS. Jesus gave this word following His Resurrection.

"And he said, 'Yes, it was written long ago that the Messiah would suffer and die and rise from the dead on the third day. It was also written that this message would be proclaimed in THE AUTHORITY OF HIS NAME TO ALL THE NATIONS ... You are WITNESSES of ALL THESE THINGS. And now I will send the Holy Spirit, just as my Father promised. But stay here in the city until the Holy Spirit comes and FILLS YOU WITH POWER FROM HEAVEN." (Luke 24:46-49 NLT)

A witness is only as good as the truth of his word, and their witness that Jesus came to DO GOOD and HEAL

---

[28] G3140

those OPPRESSED OF THE DEVIL was to be proclaimed to ALL NATIONS and they had the AUTHORITY OF HIS NAME to do it.

They had His authority but also the SAME POWER to "preach the word with signs following." What the Holy Spirit had done through Christ, the Holy Spirit would also do through His disciples because He *must* testify of all that Christ did, all He is doing, and all He will do.

Yesterday, Today, and Forever.

Chapter 3

The Church of Acts

Comedian Michael Jr. does a funny skit about Jesus' younger brother "James," living up to family expectations. "Why can't you do what Jesus' would do? He turned water into wine." Laughter is medicine for the soul, it says in Proverbs.[1]

In fact, Jesus' family is mentioned several times in the gospels and his mother and his aunt as seeing Him crucified.[2] However, unnoticed by many readers, Mary, the mother of our Lord, is also mentioned in the beginning of Acts when they tarried in the upper room, waiting the coming of the Holy Spirit.

"Then returned they unto Jerusalem from the mount called Olivet, which is from Jerusalem a sabbath day's journey. And when they were come in, they went up into an upper room, where abode both Peter, and James, and John, and Andrew, Philip, and Thomas, Bartholomew, and Matthew, James the son of Alphaeus, and Simon Zelotes, and Judas the brother of James. These all continued with one accord in prayer and supplication, with the women, and Mary the mother of Jesus, and with his brethren." (Acts 1:12-14)

I must pause and reflect on the joy of her soul at seeing her son alive after she'd witnessed His cruel death, and on her knowing that the word of the angel, thirty-three

---

[1] Pr 17:22

[2] Mt 12:46; Mk 6:3; Jn 19:25

years ago, had come true and been fulfilled in that moment. Also, how meaningful that she gathered with these men who had followed Him faithfully, who were PASSIONATE about Him, to receive the promise of the Holy Spirit.[3]

How amazing that is!

I think we've assumed it was the eleven, a meager sad group, and no more. But, in fact there were about 120 people, men *and* women, His mom, His brothers, included. All of them, in expectation of the fulfillment of His promise for the Comforter. And why wouldn't they believe the Holy Spirit would come? Every word He'd spoken to them had come true. He'd told them it would far in advance of His crucifixion to give them comfort and help them believe.[4]

Maybe they didn't fully know what would happen next, what the advent of the Holy Spirit would be like. Then again, they had seen Jesus DO GOOD and HEAL those OPPRESSED OF THE DEVIL. They had been sent out before Him to CAST OUT DEVILS IN HIS NAME.

Plus, John the Baptist had referred to the upcoming event as a baptism of fire.[5] Had they heard that? Did they remember? It's impossible to say.

One truth shines clearly, they were united in their purpose, united in their love for Christ, and their expectation that the Holy Spirit would fall on them and the POWER of the Resurrection would work in them and through them with miracles.

"And when the day of Pentecost was fully come, they were all with ONE ACCORD in one place." (Acts 2:1)

Albert Barnes' Notes on the Bible says of the Day of

---

[3] Act 1:4-5

[4] Jn 14:29

[5] Mt 3:11; Lk 3:16

Pentecost: "This fact is mentioned, that the time of the Pentecost had come, or fully arrived, to account for what is related afterward, that there were so many strangers and foreigners present. The promised influences of the Spirit were withheld until the greatest possible number of Jews should be present at Jerusalem at the same time, and thus an opportunity be afforded of preaching the gospel to vast multitudes in the very place where the Lord Jesus was crucified, and also an opportunity be afforded of sending the gospel by them into distant parts of the earth."

This should make sense to us. What were Jesus' words before He ascended?

"But ye shall receive power, after that the Holy Ghost is come upon you: and YE SHALL BE WITNESSES UNTO ME both in Jerusalem, and in all Judaea, and in Samaria, and unto the uttermost part of the earth." (Acts 1:8)

Once more, He stressed their purpose – TO BE WITNESSES OF HIM. But notice, it's AFTER the Holy Ghost has come upon them.

They could go out and talk about Jesus, as is. But Jesus wanted them to have the POWER, the DUNAMIS of God, first. **He wanted them to speak with His AUTHORITY and to DO GOOD and HEAL like He did.**

In doing that, they gave proof of His Resurrection. All the world, from the area where they lived unto the UTTERMOST PART OF THE EARTH, would SEE in the POWER that worked through them that He lives! Otherwise, who would believe a group of Jesus' fanatics that could do no more than swear their words were true? No, the GREATER THINGS must come, and in that time, in that place, among those people was the fulfillment of all that Jesus came to DO.

On the foundation of CHRIST as the Anointed One was the church built for its members to GO into all the world and PREACH THE GOOD NEWS.[6] But don't stop there, because SIGNS *will* follow it.[7]

"And suddenly there came a sound from heaven as of a rushing mighty wind, and it filled all the house where they were sitting. And there appeared unto them cloven tongues like as of fire, and it sat upon each of them. And they were all filled with the Holy Ghost, and began to speak with other tongues, as the Spirit gave them utterance." (Acts 2:2-4)

Someone pointed out that it says a "SOUND from heaven as of a rushing mighty wind" and that doesn't necessarily mean there was an actual wind. I find that interesting. Whether this is the case or not, though, the Holy Spirit filled the room, and it is of interest to me that He sat on each of them individually. He was corporate and personal at once.

This is God's heart. He united them but also spoke to each one. Then having been filled, they could not remain silent.

"And there were dwelling at Jerusalem Jews, devout men, out of every nation under heaven. Now when this was noised abroad, the multitude came together, and were confounded, because that every man HEARD THEM SPEAK IN HIS OWN LANGUAGE. And they were all amazed and marvelled, saying one to another, Behold, are not all these which speak Galilaeans? And how hear we every man IN OUR OWN TONGUE, WHEREIN WE WERE BORN? Parthians,

---

[6] Mk 16:15
[7] Mk 16:17-18

and Medes, and Elamites, and the dwellers in Mesopotamia, and in Judaea, and Cappadocia, in Pontus, and Asia, Phrygia, and Pamphylia, in Egypt, and in the parts of Libya about Cyrene, and strangers of Rome, Jews and proselytes, Cretes and Arabians, WE DO HEAR THEM SPEAK IN OUR TONGUES THE WONDERFUL WORKS OF GOD." (Acts 2:5-11)

Today, we aren't surprised when our neighbor can speak a second language. Many people do, either from birth or through study. But back then, the fact these were men from Galilee speaking a wide multitude of languages that they shouldn't know was remarkable. This, in itself, is of utmost importance.

But we should also understand that here are 120 men and women speaking SO LOUDLY that everyone on the street heard them. This was not a quiet, austere experience. This was FIRE, uncontainable.

The visual picture is relevant. In 2019, within the U.S., there were 46,706 wildfires, destroying over 4.6 million acres.[8] Some 1.1 million men and women are trained to fight them.[9]

Fire is an incredible force that can destroy a home in three or four minutes.[10]

How much greater is the power of God, which can HEAL, and DELIVER from demonic OPPRESSION, power that can raise our Savior out of hell? Hear the God of creation speak:

"Behold, I am the LORD, the God of all flesh: is there any thing too hard for me?" (Jeremiah 32:27)

---

[8] https://www.iii.org/fact-statistic/facts-statistics-wildfires

[9] https://www.firerescue1.com/fire-products/firefighter-accountability/articles/top-12-firefighter-facts-ZNtSlYDCA0tbwJ2P/

[10] https://www.angieslist.com/articles/why-newer-homes-burn-faster.htm

Perhaps, it isn't His ABILITY that stops you from taking hold, though. Perhaps, it is His willingness. Ask yourself this – Would our heavenly Father send His Son to earth to remove the devil's OPPRESSION, to DO GOOD, yet once the crucifixion and ascension were done, sit back and relax?

He didn't do that. He sent the Holy Spirit to continue to TESTIFY of His GOODNESS, to change hearts, renew minds, and heal bodies. To show His glory to all corners of the earth. Forever.

Salvation had come, and strength, and the kingdom of God, and the POWER of the ANOINTED ONE, and nothing on earth would ever be the same.[11]

This is that.

The people listening to the ruckus on the day of Pentecost were full of wonder at the noise they heard, and I can understand why. Imagine you've come to observe Pentecost, or maybe you're doing business in the city. You've done this many times before and never seen or heard such a racket.

"What's goin' on here? These people have been drinking," the onlookers said.[12]

This amuses me. I've watched a lot of reality crime shows over the years and have yet to see a drunk man or woman speak fluently in any language, much less a large group of them as described here in Acts.

But Peter. Oh, Peter. I love Peter. No one was more PASSIONATE for Christ. Peter set them straight.

"For these are not drunken, as ye suppose, seeing it is

---

[11] Rev 12:10

[12] Act 2:12-13

but the third hour of the day. But THIS IS THAT which was spoken by the prophet Joel." (Acts 2:15-16)

This is THAT. That POWER prophesied. That JESUS, who God raised from the dead. That FIRE of the Holy Ghost, spoken of by John. That AUTHORITY to GO into the world and make disciples.

This is that commission to be WITNESSES unto the far parts of the earth.

This is that, which HEALED and SAVED and set people FREE.

This is Him, who you crucified and considered dead and gone. This is that RESURRECTION, which rolled the stone away. This is He, who appeared to us many times after His death, who spoke life and truth and peace.

"Ye men of Israel, hear these words; Jesus of Nazareth, a man APPROVED OF GOD AMONG YOU BY MIRACLES AND WONDERS AND SIGNS, WHICH GOD DID BY HIM in the midst of you, as ye yourselves also know ... Whom God hath raised up, HAVING LOOSED the pains of death: because it was not possible that he should be holden of it ... THIS JESUS hath God raised up, whereof WE ALL ARE WITNESSES. Therefore being by the right hand of God exalted, and having received of the Father the promise of the Holy Ghost, HE HATH SHED FORTH THIS, WHICH YE NOW SEE AND HEAR." (Acts 2:22, 24, 32-33)

This is that. That God. That Spirit. That sacrifice. That victory.

"This is your freedom," Peter said.

"Repent, and be baptized every one of you in the name of Jesus Christ for the remission of sins, and YE SHALL

RECEIVE the gift of the Holy Ghost. FOR THE PROMISE IS UNTO YOU, AND TO YOUR CHILDREN, AND TO ALL THAT ARE AFAR OFF, even as many as the Lord our God shall call." (Acts 2:38-39)

This is that change you've been looking for. That HEALING you've been seeking. That DELIVERANCE you've searched to find. This is GOD ACCOMPLISHED in men. This is CHRIST, the Messiah.

This is salvation from sins. This is the gift of the Holy Ghost. This is the church.

How we long to see Him work in power amongst us still. Who doesn't seek the Lord when a loved one is gravely ill? Who fails to pray over a sick child? Who sees a grandmother pass away and doesn't picture her in heaven? Even those without God do that. We, the church, should desire these signs and wonders even more. Greater, we are filled with the Spirit and, being filled, should WITNESS of His delivering power.

We cannot limit the goodness of God to the four gospels. We cannot terminate it in the book of Acts. **The church should be where anyone can come to be made WHOLE.** This was God's will in Acts, and it is God's will still. Though the pages of the Bible reach an ending, the truths in it do not.

We are called to "ACTS" LIKE HIM. We are to turn a hurting world, in every sense of the word, to a loving, forgiving, healing Jesus.

About 3,000 people were saved that day, after Peter's preaching.

"And fear came upon every soul: and many WONDERS and SIGNS were done BY THE APOSTLES."[13]

---

[13] Act 2:43

Because the Holy Spirit had come, and friend, at no time has He left or lifted His hands from the earth since then.

The only hindrance to the next miracle is within ourselves.

Chapter 4

A Greater Church

There I was, writing *"A Good Life,"* when God directed me toward the book of Acts. He spoke five Scriptures out of their usual order, in a pattern that showed the development of these men, who'd followed Him so faithfully as they became the early church. One Scripture stood out from the others in my heart, but to understand it, we must reverse a bit.

Acts 3 begins the story of a remarkable healing that clearly was of some note since it is detailed separately. We'll read verses 1-10.

"Now Peter and John went up together into the temple at the hour of prayer, being the ninth hour. And a certain man lame from his mother's womb was carried, whom they laid daily at the gate of the temple which is called Beautiful, to ask alms of them that entered into the temple; Who seeing Peter and John about to go into the temple asked an alms. And Peter, fastening his eyes upon him with John, said, Look on us. And he gave heed unto them, expecting to receive something of them. Then Peter said, Silver and gold have I none; BUT SUCH AS I HAVE GIVE I THEE: In the name of Jesus Christ of Nazareth rise up and walk. And he took him by the right hand, and lifted him up: and immediately his feet and ankle bones received strength. And he leaping up stood, and walked, and entered with them into the temple, walking, and leaping, and praising God. And ALL THE PEOPLE SAW HIM walking and praising God: AND THEY KNEW THAT IT WAS HE which sat for alms at the Beautiful gate of the temple: and they were filled with

wonder and amazement at that which had happened unto him." (Acts 3:1-10)

Here's a man that everyone knew. It says he was laid DAILY at the temple gate. This means someone placed him there because he couldn't walk, had never walked. He was a figure in the community. He's also in a public place, at the place of worship, nonetheless.

Peter and John had gone there to pray. The man was there to beg for alms. Something he did daily, remember? Yet when he asked alms of Peter and John, something supernatural happened. The verse doesn't say exactly what, but I imagine the Holy Spirit grabbed Peter and caused him to act, because minutes later, the lame man is leaping and praising God, totally healed.

Don't miss Peter's words to him:

"Such as I have give I thee: In the name of Jesus Christ of Nazareth rise up and walk." (Acts 3:6)

What did he have? The POWER of the Holy Ghost and the AUTHORITY of the name of Jesus to do as Jesus did – to HEAL those OPPRESSED OF THE DEVIL.

The power of faith

Surrounded by the people, who marveled at such a remarkable healing, Peter reiterates that it was the name of Jesus, now risen from the dead, who made the man sound. In his words, he includes an important truth.

"And his name [Jesus] THROUGH FAITH IN HIS NAME hath made this man strong, whom ye see and know: yea, THE FAITH WHICH IS BY HIM hath given him this perfect

soundness in the presence of you all." (Acts 3:16)

It was FAITH IN JESUS' NAME that healed the lame man. Peter through faith expected God to fulfill His promise – to heal, to save, and to deliver.

Jesus had said whatever they asked in His name, the Father would do.[1] He'd also told them, *"And these signs SHALL FOLLOW THEM THAT BELIEVE; IN MY NAME shall they"* cast out devils and bring healing to the sick.[2]

But it was their FAITH that made the POWER work.

At the same time, Jesus' name is not a magic wand to be waved whenever anyone feels like it. That is not faith, and I don't want to give you that impression. Two men, exorcists, tried to cast out devils in Jesus' name, and the devils proved stronger.[3]

God desires godly vessels, without pride in their hearts, who will submit their will to Him.[4] He desires faith in the words He's spoken and in what HIS NAME has accomplished.[5]

The concept of faith confuses people when it is so simple. **At its heart, faith believes in God's character.** It knows He is love and wants to bless, heal, and prosper His people.[6] Faith believes in the authority of Jesus' name, knowing Jesus' defeated Satan.[7] It believes God inhabits and works through His people. A man or woman of faith has tuned their spiritual ears to God's voice and dedicates all their actions toward protecting that relationship.

What we desire, we will seek after and we will work

---

1 Jn 16:23-24
2 Mk 16:17
3 Act 19:13-16
4 Jas 4:7
5 Heb 11:6
6 1Jn 4:8
7 Eph 1:20-21; Php 2:9; Col 2:15

to protect.[8] If the move of God's Spirit is truly our heart's wish, then we will spend time with Him to know Him and we will set aside everything else.[9] Things of entertainment – TV, cell phones, sports games – become less important than holding onto the move of God in us.

Faith is developed. Faith grows, and that growth takes time.[10] No farmer plants a seed on the 18th and harvests the crop on the 19th. Instead, what I can't believe for today, I spend time building my faith in. By reading the Word of God over and over, I will know for sure the answer belongs to me.[11]

At my weakest point, I would say, "This is the day the Lord has made. I will rejoice and be glad in it," then go into the bathroom and be sick all over again.[12] I didn't believe what I'd said one bit, so it didn't manifest itself to me. But as I continued in this word,[13] one day I knew that I knew that *today* was a day of joy and gladness given to me by God. Even if I still had stomach troubles, my body reacting to imagined stress, I had a good day because I had faith in God for it.

Faith requires standing in one place until you see the answer. That is why Ephesians refers to it as a shield.[14] Faith is taking the offense, pushing back against the "fiery darts" that come toward you.

What does it mean by "fiery darts?" These are the words of other people, the doubts in your mind, or the troubled sight in front of you. I had to see myself free from

---

[8] Mt 7:7
[9] Gal 5:24-25
[10] Mk 4:31-32; Jud 1:20
[11] Ps 1:2; Mt 17:20-21
[12] Ps 118:24
[13] Jas 1:25
[14] Eph 6:13-14, 16

fear to become free from fear, and I had to strive for it by faith, believing God was walking with me, though the world around me seemed far different.

Peter and John spoke FAITH IN JESUS' NAME to the lame man. They knew Jesus. They knew what He'd said He'd do, He would! And the lame man, strengthened by the power of the Holy Spirit, had faith to obey and rise and walk.

But do you know he could have sat there and refused? He could have said, "I can't do that. I was born this way."

Thank God, he didn't.

A Greater Work

Matthew 24 is a passage of Scripture that, being honest, I've avoided like the plague. End-time events, or writings about end-time events, has always scared the living daylights out of me. This goes back to my teen years when it was fashionable for youth group leaders to show these "what will happen after the rapture" type videos. As if it would hurl teens toward the altar.

One such video turned me off studying anything prophetic for good. I was having none of that ever again, to the point that whenever a speaker came to the church and that was the topic, I'd leave.

God isn't in the business of instilling fear. At no time does He need fear's help to make His point. Being young (and afraid), I couldn't see that. When I read this passage today, I see God's truths about love and deliverance instead. I encourage you to study it in a modern translation. It really is marvelous.

But the entire discourse was brought about because of the disciples' questions after viewing the temple.[15] The

---

[15] Mt 24:3

fact they asked questions about the future tells us that they'd grown in knowledge. Jesus had spoken of His upcoming death and subsequent Resurrection more than once.[16] Here, He warns them of what persecution they'd suffer.[17] Though what would happen in just days would throw them into temporary chaos, the Scripture tells us that afterward they thought on Jesus' words and finally understood them.[18]

So, when the events of Acts 4 happened, neither Peter nor John were too surprised. The lame man had drawn attention to them. Peter had preached about Jesus' Resurrection, some 5,000 people getting saved, and the Sadducees, overhearing it all, seized them and tossed them in jail.[19] They wouldn't have any more talk about people rising from the dead.

The next day, however, gathered together to decide what to do about it, they made the mistake of questioning Peter. What did he think he was doing? Who gave him the right?

"And when they had set them [Peter, John, and the lame man] in the midst, they asked, BY WHAT POWER, OR BY WHAT NAME, have ye done this?" (Acts 4:7)

Have you ever asked something and regretted it? Either the question was stupid, and you knew the answer already, or you asked the one person you shouldn't have? Perhaps this is just me, but I've often said, "I don't know what that means, and don't explain it." I do not need an explanation for everything.

---

[16] Mt 12:40; Jn 2:19

[17] Mt 24:9

[18] Lk 24:8; Jn 12:6

[19] Act 4:1, 4

Well, Peter, filled with the Holy Spirit, had an answer that made the religious leaders wish they hadn't asked.

"Rulers and elders of the people, yesterday A GOOD DEED was done. Someone who WAS SICK WAS HEALED. If you're asking us how this happened, I want all of you and all of the people of Israel to know this man standing in front of you—obviously in good health—was HEALED BY THE AUTHORITY OF JESUS OF NAZARETH, THE ANOINTED ONE. This is the same Jesus whom you crucified and whom God raised from the dead. He is 'the stone that you builders rejected who has become the very stone that holds together the entire foundation' on which a new temple is being built. There is no one else who can rescue us, and there is NO OTHER NAME UNDER HEAVEN given to any human BY WHOM WE MAY BE RESCUED." (Acts 4:8-13 VOICE)

"The AUTHORITY of Jesus, the DUNAMIS of God, the FORCE RESIDING IN HIM, healed this man," he said. "Jesus alone did this."

What a powerful response in the face of disbelief! It calls to mind a commentary I read about the apostle Paul's words to the Galatian church. In chapter 3, verse 1, he takes them to task for their disbelief and disobedience.

"O foolish Galatians, who hath bewitched you, that ye should not obey the truth, before whose eyes Jesus Christ hath been evidently set forth, crucified among you? This only would I learn of you, Received ye the Spirit by the works of the law, or by the hearing of faith?" (Galatians 3:1-2)

David Guzik's Enduring Word Commentary says, "Their vision of Jesus Christ and Him crucified has become cloudy. They no longer see Him and His work on the cross as the center of their Christian lives, now it is JESUS PLUS ..."

There is no Jesus plus.

Jesus plus our job, our bank account, our years in church. Jesus plus charity work, generous contributions, an hour in prayer every day at five a.m. As if He needs our help. No, He needs our faith.

Not, Jesus in our pocket, and we pull Him out like a repair kit. Jesus, hocus pocus. Wave Him over your problem and recite a few psalms.

"Jesus plus" implies He's not enough. Run, quick because Jesus can't handle the mountain we've started to climb.

It sounds ridiculous, but the Galatians mixed faith with carnal works and forgot about the time-altering moment when faith became faith in the first place.

There's no Jesus formula.

"Buy now, the five-step program toward success!"

"Take these spiritual vitamins and call me in the morning."

No, faith requires living in God's Word. It's burying your head in the water of the Good Book and drinking deep.

My mom tells a story about a woman who meditated on Acts 10:38 so long that when the grocery store clerk said, "That'll be $10.38," she recited the verse instead. That's awesome. We should be that full.

Full of Jesus alone. Our every breath, knowing that He answers prayers spoken in faith. Faith that's grown in us because we've spent so much time in His Word, we've totally overlooked the distractions. We're focused, instead, on the Author and Finisher.[20]

He started the ball rolling and has provided the happy ending already.

---

[20] Heb 12:2

Jesus, singular, enduring the cross, in spite of all the voices howling around him. In spite of the fear lumped in His throat, knowing He had to die and be disconnected from the Father, He saw the Resurrection as completed.

Jesus, victorious. Consider that next time you want to give up.

Again, I remember something David Guzik's Enduring Word Commentary said. Of Hebrews 12:3, he states, "But they should consider Him who endured such hostility from sinners against Himself, and be encouraged, not discouraged, knowing that they are following in the footsteps of Jesus."

There is no greater calling for the PASSIONATE CHURCH.

The religious leaders marveled at Peter and John because they were uneducated men. No one who hadn't studied the Scriptures extensively, no one who'd come from peasant towns, no lowly fisherman should be able to talk like that.

Except, what had Jesus said when He called Peter, there on the shores of Galilee?

"Follow me, and I will make you fishers of men." (Matthew 4:19)

God saw Peter's heart before he'd ever turned loose of the net. He knew what he could become through the power of the Holy Spirit.

This builds such hope in me that whenever I feel insufficient and small, God's perspective is so much grander. What an example we have in Peter, whose *"extraordinary confidence"* astounded priests and scholars.[21]

---

[21] Act 4:13 VOICE

They saw his FAITH, though they didn't know it. They heard the POWER of the Holy Spirit in his words. They were looking at a man, who believed in God with all his being. He depended on JESUS ALONE.

Even greater, there beside him and John was a man, born lame, standing healed and whole, a WITNESS to the healing power of Jesus' name.

"And beholding the man which was healed standing with them, they could say nothing against it." (Acts 4:14)

Every time I read that verse, I want to leap. "See! See! You can't argue with a MIRACLE. Can you?"

Here was a GREATER WORK. **Here was God in manifestation.** On this rock of revelation the church will triumph over hell.[22]

The ANOINTING came to HEAL all those OPPRESSED OF THE DEVIL. Being lame was the devil's work. Walking and leaping and praising God was God's. Facing the Sadducees armed with such confidence was God's. Having words to speak that they couldn't argue against was God's.

Jesus had spoken this prophecy.

"But before all these, they shall lay their hands on you, and persecute you, delivering you up to the synagogues, and into prisons, being brought before kings and rulers for my name's sake. And it shall TURN TO YOU FOR A TESTIMONY. Settle it therefore in your hearts, not to meditate before what ye shall answer: For I will give you A MOUTH AND WISDOM, which all your adversaries shall not be able to gainsay nor resist." (Luke 21:12-15)

---

[22] Mt 16:18 VOICE

The Passion Translation states verses 14-15 this way: *"Yet determine in your hearts not to prepare for your own defense. Simply speak with the words of wisdom that I will give you that moment, and none of your persecutors will be able to withstand the grace and wisdom that comes from your mouths."*

No one will be able to argue with you. This happened to Peter right then. The religious leaders couldn't say one word about the results. Even after deliberation, the best they could do was warn him not to speak in "that name" again.

Little did they know that the story was just beginning.

Chapter 5

An Active Church

Greece, under the leadership of Alexander III of Macedon, known by most as Alexander the Great, created one of the largest kingdoms in the world. Spanning some 3,000 miles, it stretched from Egypt to Persia, circling the Mediterranean Sea. Alexander the Great was undefeated in his reign, going down in history as one of the greatest soldiers of all time.

Yet for all his achievements, Alexander died at age 32, and his kingdom split into fractions. The memory of his name and his amazing conquests couldn't hold the kingdom together.[1]

Jesus told a parable to his disciples, which is recorded in Matthew 20. In it, the owner of a vineyard was looking for laborers to bring in the harvest, so he went to town at dawn and hired a group of men, promising them a penny's wage. Later that morning, he hired another group, and late afternoon, still a third. Finally, the day almost ended, he sought out a fourth. He posed them a question, which speaks to my heart.

"And about the eleventh hour he went out, and found others standing idle, and saith unto them, WHY STAND YE HERE ALL THE DAY IDLE? They say unto him, Because no man hath hired us. He saith unto them, GO YE ALSO INTO THE VINEYARD; and whatsoever is right, that shall ye receive." (Matthew 20:6-7)

---

1 https://en.wikipedia.org/wiki/Alexander_the_Great; https://www.ushistory.org/civ/5g.asp

These words came to me from the Holy Spirit, and I saw in them the truth. The church has been given a mandate to GO into the world with the GOOD NEWS that Jesus SAVES, HEALS, and DELIVERS.[2] Yet the majority stand around IDLE, waiting for some thunderbolt, some spiritual shove to shake them out of their lethargy. Comfortable in their pews, they explain away the book of Acts, stories so pivotal to all we are supposed to be.

It is there, we read the church was first called Christians. This is of tremendous importance, yet we have failed to understand it.

The church world was astir. Gentiles were being saved and filled with the Holy Spirit, a promise previously available only to the Jews. News of the demonstration of God's POWER changing lives at Antioch reached Jerusalem, and Barnabas and Saul were sent to minister there.[3] They stayed for a year, and it was the effect of their teaching about Christ that caused the name to be used.

They were called followers of THE ANOINTED ONE, not just spokesmen, but men flowing in the POWER OF GOD, PASSIONATE for CHRIST. **They exhibited GOD'S NATURE to the world.** It was the GREATER WORKS that happened there, their ZEAL for the message of the gospel, that made others label them that way.

We don't understand zeal. It is defined as "fervor for a person, cause, or object; eager desire or endeavor; enthusiastic diligence; ardor." In the Greek, it means "heat."[4] It comes from a word meaning "to boil."[5]

"And his disciples remembered that it was written,

---

[2] Mk 16:15-17

[3] Act 11:21-22, 26

[4] G2205

[5] Vincent's Word Studies, John 2:17

The zeal of thine house hath eaten me up." (John 2:17)

Being a Christian should be more than strange people who attend church. It should show a difference in lifestyle, a fervor, a HEAT for the things of God. The ANOINTED ONE reigns in us! **We should shine as someone who has the ANSWER.** Our prayers should be EFFECTIVE and the answers we receive, noticed.[6]

After Jesus ascended into the heavens, the group gathered there, Jesus' disciples, his brothers, and his mother, gazed into the sky well after He'd vanished from view, and a pair of angels appeared and asked them a question.

"Ye men of Galilee, WHY STAND YE GAZING UP INTO HEAVEN? this same Jesus, which is taken up from you into heaven, shall so come in like manner as ye have seen him go into heaven." (Acts 1:11)

"Why are you standing here? Go!"

This isn't a club we've joined that comes with a badge for our jacket and a nice-looking cap. We are ACTIVE PARTICIPANTS. We hold in our hearts the keys to divine life, to incredible life that can HEAL and SET FREE and MEND HEARTS. This life in us DESTROYED THE WORKS OF THE DEVIL and reigns TRIUMPHANT over hell.

We cannot help but be CONSUMED with that.

DUNAMIS, God's EXCELLENCE and integrity, can change governments. The FORCE of HIS POWER can raise the dead and do MIGHTY WORKS. Jesus' name is above all other names. With it comes MORAL power and all of God's RESOURCES.

---

[6] Jas 5:16

Late 19th century minister, George Müller opened his first orphanage to prove God would supply all his needs. He never asked for donations, never publicized his work, and more than once refused to even share their end-of-the-year profit and loss. He wanted no one to be able to say they'd given through any physical knowledge.

Time and time again, people would show up at his door and say, "God told me to give you this." Frequently, they were at their emptiest, no money to pay staff or purchase food or other necessities. Once, he sat the children at the table for the meal and someone showed up, unannounced, at the door with what they needed.

Of his dependence on our heavenly Father for resources, he said:

"This plan may be despised by some, ridiculed by others, and considered insufficient by a third class of persons, but under every trial and difficulty, we find prayer and faith to be our universal remedy; and, after having experienced for half a century their efficacy, we purpose, by God's help, to *continue* waiting upon Him, in order to show to an ungodly world, and to a doubting Church, that the Living God is still able and willing to answer prayer, and that it is the joy of His heart to listen to the supplications of His children. In Psalm ix. 10, the Divine testimony regarding Jehovah is, 'They that know thy name will put their trust in Thee.' We know Him, by His grace, and do therefore put our trust in Him." ("Answers to Prayer" by George Müller)

If the church as a whole would grasp that, instead of trafficking in fear and disbelief, instead of being known for our sins and criticisms, what MIRACLES we would see. What BOLDNESS we would have. Because released from their bonds and told not to speak Jesus' name anymore, the church of Acts gathered together and prayed a prayer that weights my heart.

"And now, Lord, behold their threatenings: and grant unto thy servants, that with ALL BOLDNESS they may speak thy word, BY STRETCHING FORTH THINE HAND TO HEAL; and that SIGNS AND WONDERS MAY BE DONE by the name of thy holy child Jesus." (Acts 4:29-30)

Not, "Save us, Lord. We're in trouble here." Nor, "What are we going to do now?"

But ALL BOLDNESS. "Make us louder. Make us stronger. Perform miracles through us. Fill us with your POWER, and let the whole world know Jesus has conquered death!"

God can handle the pressure, and He takes care of His own, those who walk by faith, EXPECTANT. That really is the heart of faith. We get what we expect, and with God, more than we expect.

He is *"exceeding abundantly ABOVE all that we can ask or think."* Notice, why. It is *"according to the POWER that worketh in us."*[7] Holy Ghost power. DUNAMIS. The NATURE OF GOD. His MIGHT and RICHES. It's time for us to believe it.

Being Like Jesus

Jesus attended a wedding with his mother in Cana of Galilee. This seems like such an ordinary thing to do. His mom was invited, and it says, He and His disciples as well.

When the feast ran out of wine, Mary placed her faith in Him to solve the problem.

Here, I must pause and consider things. God had

---

[7] Eph 3:20

chosen Mary out of all the girls in the land. He'd obviously saw in her faith in the impossible. How fitting then that she would become the instigation for Jesus' first miracle.

The Scripture says Mary "pondered," or meditated on, what had happened to her, as well as on the events in His life.[8] In light of that, I can imagine, at this point, she knew many things that only a mother would know. She'd obviously figured out the POWER of God was with Him.

"And both Jesus was called, and his disciples, to the marriage. And when they wanted wine, the mother of Jesus saith unto him, They have no wine. Jesus saith unto her, Woman, what have I to do with thee? mine hour is not yet come. His mother saith unto the servants, WHATSOEVER HE SAITH UNTO YOU, DO IT." (John 2:2-5)

God responds to faith. Mary spoke in faith, and a miracle happened. It really is that simple.

We must also notice that God made the BEST wine. No subpar, second-best results ever come from Him.[9] He is Alpha and Omega, the beginning AND the end.[10] He sees things through to completion with the highest quality outcome.

His heart is full of love for people. **He wants the best life for every man and woman.** He wants us free from physical and mental ailments, from addictions, bad habits, and all other types of bondage. He is compassion in its purest form. Where we humanly fall short, He never will.

One day, Jesus was dining with the dregs of society, and the Pharisees took exception to it. The Voice Translation puts it this way: *"When the Pharisees' scribes saw who*

---

[8] Lk 2:19, 51

[9] Jn 2:10

[10] Rev 1:8, 11

shared the table with Jesus, they were QUICK TO CRITICIZE."[11]

I've said this many times before on social media, but anytime you find yourself thinking, feeling, or speaking from a negative point-of-view, then you need to reevaluate. And lest you think I'm not speaking personally, I totally am, but I saw the damage it did to my day, the unhappiness it engendered in the long run, and decided it wasn't worth it.

We cannot use the Scriptures as a weapon for our hate. They are not meant to frighten or condemn anyone but are the fullness of God's love.

Jesus came for sinners, for the broken and messed up.[12] If you think you are righteous under your own strength, you aren't. Just as it was impossible to find salvation under the precepts of the Mosaic law, it is impossible to prove yourself good enough through charitable deeds or personal success to bypass the foundation of God's Word and then have any true happiness.

Going to church doesn't put you in a higher class of people. It means you've chosen to become like Christ and to overcome your shortcomings through Him. Being righteousness, which means being in clean-standing with God or in a "right" place, cannot be earned.[13] It must, however, BE LIVED.

The righteous are to follow Jesus' example, and Jesus came to DO GOOD. The church's mission is, therefore, to DO GOOD. Even if you dismiss the blood-bought provision of healing in its entirety, you, as a member of the body of Christ, should be DOING GOOD

And let me say it again—Jesus never condemned

---

[11] Mk 2:16

[12] Mk 2:17

[13] Rm 5:17-18

anyone. He showed love.

"There is therefore now NO CONDEMNATION to them which are in Christ Jesus, WHO WALK NOT AFTER THE FLESH, but after the Spirit." (Romans 8:1)

The word "condemnation" means a damning verdict.[14] In other words, you've been judged and found guilty. But there is NO CONDEMNATION to those who follow the guidance of the Holy Spirit.

The Message Bible gives this passage a phenomenal meaning:

"With the arrival of Jesus, the Messiah, that fateful dilemma is resolved. Those who enter into Christ's being-here-for-us no longer have to live under a continuous, low-lying black cloud. A NEW POWER is in operation. The Spirit of life in Christ, like a strong wind, has magnificently cleared the air, freeing you from a fated lifetime of brutal tyranny at the hands of sin and death." (Romans 8:1 MSG)

This is the GOOD that Jesus came to do. He came to free man from SIN and OPPRESSION, from the consequences of wrong choices, from REACTING to others in hate and frustration. Jesus didn't criticize those who sought Him. He guided with love, and He set an example of compassion to His disciples, the men who would become the CHURCH.

He bid them to PRAY for people and share His compassion with the world. **We are to be PASSIONATE to love others at the same magnitude that Jesus was.**

"But when he [Jesus] saw the multitudes, he was

---

[14] G2631

moved with compassion on them, because they fainted, and were scattered abroad, as sheep having no shepherd. Then saith he unto his disciples, The harvest truly is plenteous, but the labourers are few; Pray ye therefore the Lord of the harvest, that he will send forth labourers into his harvest." (Matthew 9:36-38)

David Guzik's Enduring Word Commentary says of these verses: "So, we are to pray to the Lord of the harvest that He would send out laborers. But we can only really pray this in sincerity if we pray with an ear open to hearing Him tell us, 'You go into the harvest!'"

This is sobering. We don't pray, "Lord, send someone else," but "God, send me." Absent of pride and arrogance, absent of skin color or nationality, absent of trust in any schooling, education, or bank account. We stop thinking of ourselves and GO out to ALL NATIONS to DO GOOD. We go in Jesus' name to HEAL – the heart, the mind, the body – to SET CAPTIVES FREE of the OPPRESSION that binds them.

Here's the thing, though ... Being SENT does not necessarily mean "into the mission field in a faraway country." God will use you right where you are, in your circle of influence. Every, single day is an opportunity to touch someone, to become a laborer for the harvest. This doesn't mean you walk around with a Bible in your hand. The Bible is in your heart, where God resides. The POWER OF GOD, the NATURE of all that He is works inside you. You have His DUNAMIS and the Holy Spirit to guide your words. You have the AUTHORITY of name of Jesus over all the POWER OF THE ENEMY.

You have in you, Christ, the ANOINTED ONE, and ALL THINGS for life and godliness.

These are the words of 2 Peter 1:3.

"According as HIS DIVINE POWER hath given unto us ALL THINGS that pertain unto life and godliness, through the knowledge of him that hath called us to glory and virtue." (2 Peter 1:3)

His divine POWER, His DUNAMIS, God's NATURE, His EXCELLENCE, His INFLUENCE, all of the MIGHT of HIS NAME has given to us, the believers. We have ALL THINGS needed for a powerful life and true godliness, or we could say, another word to express godliness, holiness works in us through the POWER of God.[15] We seek to be holy because He is holy, in our actions and in our words.[16]

Now add in the next verse. We'll read it in the Passion Translation.

"Everything we could ever need for life and complete devotion to God has already been deposited in us BY HIS DIVINE POWER. For all this was lavished upon us through the rich experience of knowing him who has called us by name and invited us to come to him through a glorious manifestation of his goodness. As a result of this, he has given you magnificent promises that are beyond all price, so that through the power of these tremendous promises YOU CAN EXPERIENCE PARTNERSHIP WITH THE DIVINE NATURE, by which you have escaped the corrupt desires that are of the world." (2 Peter 1:3-4)

What a marvelous reality! Having escaped the world's way of doing things, we enter into partnership with God, and through His POWER, we experience all that He is. We are no longer who we were, but we are who He has

---

[15] G2150

[16] 1Pe 1:15-16

made us to be.

A list of virtues follows these verses, giving us a picture of God's nature. It starts with faith but says faith by itself isn't enough. Because to be like God, we must combine faith with goodness, understanding, self-control, patience, godliness, and mercy. All of these things work together to make us like God. And they are all tied together with the greatest characteristic of all – love.[17]

Love that went to the utmost extreme to save people who didn't deserve it, including you and me. DIVINE LOVE and the POWER of the Holy Spirit in us causes us to THINK LIKE GOD and DO what God would do.

What God did when He sent Jesus to live a brief, sinless life and accept the hatred and unjust accusations of the very people who needed Him the most.

---

[17] 2Pe 1:5-7

Chapter 6

The Forgiving Church

The story of Jesus cursing the fig tree has been examined from many angles, but I want us to hear Jesus' words because DECIDING TO BE the church that God designed isn't enough. It's not enough to say you'll pray for people or give a substantial sum in the offering if you are lacking the most important knowledge about the working of DUNAMIS.

We have all probably heard the basics of what happened that day. Jesus cursed the fig tree because it had no fruit. He and the disciples proceeded on toward Jerusalem, and on the way home, a day later, Peter saw the tree was dried up from the roots and brought it to everyone's attention.[1]

Jesus' comments, though, seemed to seriously veer away from the fig tree.

"Therefore I say unto you, What things soever ye desire, when ye pray, believe that ye receive them, and ye shall have them. And WHEN YE STAND PRAYING, FORGIVE, if ye have ought against any: that your Father also which is in heaven may forgive you your trespasses. But IF YE DO NOT FORGIVE, neither will your Father which is in heaven forgive your trespasses." (Mark 11:24-26)

How perplexing. Though His statement speaks to us of its truths, what does forgiveness have to do with casting

---

[1] Mk 11:13-14, 20-21

mountains into the sea?[2] Well, look at 1 Corinthians 13:1-3.

"Though I speak with the tongues of men and of angels, and have not charity, I am become as sounding brass, or a tinkling cymbal. And though I have the gift of prophecy, and understand all mysteries, and all knowledge; and though I have all faith, so that I could remove mountains, AND HAVE NOT CHARITY, I AM NOTHING. And though I bestow all my goods to feed the poor, and though I give my body to be burned, and HAVE NOT CHARITY, IT PROFITETH ME NOTHING." (1 Corinthians 13:1-3)

Now "charity" in the King James is not what we think of when we read the word. In the original Greek it is the word *agape*, or the DIVINE LOVE of God.

You can be uber smart and know 12 languages, or you might speak incredible prophecies; you might have the faith to move mountains, but no matter how rich you are, how intelligent, how many degrees come after your name, no matter how entitled you feel, unless you walk in God's love—IT PROFITS NOTHING.

This is the same thought we find in Mark 11:25. Without FORGIVENESS, there is no POWER in your life. Forgiveness is the exercise of love in you. It is an act of the will, not feelings or emotions. We choose to forgive regardless of if we WANT to.

God's power is dependent on your having HIS NATURE in you. It cannot DO GOOD without faith, and faith needs *agape* love. If you have *agape,* then you will have kindness and patience and goodness, which we read in 2 Peter 1:3-4 is part of God's NATURE.

In reverse, if you are impatient, unkind, envious, and

---

[2] Mk 11:23

arrogant, if you behave unseemly, which is a word meaning inappropriately, or we could say it this way ... if you have no godliness in your actions, if you're selfish, if you even think evil of someone else ("I hope she gets hit by a bus."), if you are easily provoked, then you are cut off from the POWER OF GOD working GOOD in you or through you.

James 2:17 says, *"Faith, if it hath not works, is dead."* What kind of "works?" Well, read what came before it.

"If a brother or sister be naked, and destitute of daily food, And one of you say unto them, Depart in peace, be ye warmed and filled; notwithstanding ye give them not those things which are needful to the body; what doth it profit?" (James 2:15-16)

The "works" needed to be put into practice in verse 17 is God's *agape* expressed toward people. It's seeing the need in someone else AND DOING what God's NATURE would do. It's LOVE.

People pray for revival but make no changes in their heart. People wish to see SIGNS and WONDERS, but they hate their neighbor, that politician, or their co-worker. People CHOOSE STRIFE over FORGIVENESS and so disconnect themselves from the Holy Spirit's operation in their lives at home AND at church.

God desires UNITY. We have one God, one faith, one baptism. There is one body of Christ.[3] He urges His people to SEEK PEACE.[4] He's told us time and time again the dangers of strife.

"For where envying and strife is, there is confusion

---

[3] Eph 4:3-6

[4] Ps 34:14; 1Pe 3:11

and EVERY EVIL WORK." (James 3:16)

Or we could say it this way: "Where envying and strife is, God is not."

There is no darkness in Him.[5] There is no hatred in Him.[6] There is no evil in Him. He cannot tempt you with evil or be tempted of evil.[7] Which means GOD AND THE DEVIL DO NOT WORK TOGETHER. This is outside of His character.

God sent Jesus to DO GOOD because HE IS GOOD.[8] His power HEALS because He is HEALING.[9] To believe He needs the devil as a cohort makes Him powerless.

What did Jesus say?

"I beheld Satan as lightning fall from heaven." (Luke 10:18)

If Satan fell out of heaven to a position lower than God, then why would God sink to his level to talk to Him? In fact, a study of the Scriptures shows us that Satan prided himself on who He was. He felt entitled to God's throne, so God cast him out.[10]

God would not let him usurp His power then, and He will not allow it now either.

Here's what we fail to see. We picture things on a grand scale—God being head of all the earth and sky and the devil being our enemy. We don't realize OUR WORDS AND ACTIONS, our feeling ENTITLED to our OPINION is the root of our POWERLESSNESS.

---

[5] 1Jn 1:5
[6] 1Jn 4:8
[7] Jas 1:13
[8] Ps 52:1; Rm 2:4
[9] Ex 15:26
[10] Is 14:12-15

We wouldn't tell an unsaved man or woman to lay hands on the sick and pray the prayer of faith, yet it's perfectly okay for us to do it after we snapped at our spouse. Unforgiveness unplugs us from the POWER of God. We are no longer acting like God would act, and therefore, we won't receive answers to our prayers. We cannot expect results from our faith with hate in our heart for someone else, AND we won't be able to DO GOOD.

People focus on large-scale sins: adultery, fornication, homosexuality, murder, fraud, theft. But pull the rug over the "small" ones like taking offense. They even use "godliness" as an excuse.

"But that person does this or that wrong."

God hasn't made you their judge. In fact, Jesus spoke against making judgment.[11] Plus, tell me this. When did Jesus ever do that? Did He refuse to raise Lazarus because Martha was too full of worry and frustration? No, facing the tomb, He wept over their unbelief.[12]

Mary said, "If you'd been here, he wouldn't have died."[13]

The people who'd tagged along said, "He can heal the blind, but not save Lazarus?"[14]

Martha said, "Lord, by now, he smells. He's been dead four days!"[15]

But Jesus, tears in His eyes, said: *"Said I not unto thee, that, if thou wouldest believe, thou shouldest see the glory of God?"*[16]

If Jesus had waited for perfect people to heal, they

---

[11] Mt 7:1-2
[12] Jn 11:15
[13] Jn 11:32
[14] Jn 11:37
[15] Jn 11:39
[16] Jn 11:40

wouldn't have needed healing, and He wouldn't have had to die on the cross and spend three days and nights in hell. But they weren't, and they did, and despite their sins, He gave Himself as sacrifice and rose victorious.

Thanks be to God.

No Mighty Works

If you put diesel fuel in an unleaded gasoline engine, you will destroy the engine. You can sit behind the wheel and scream and yell at it, you can even put the key in the ignition, but the engine will never crank. In this same manner, you can decide to follow Jesus' example, you are going to DO GOOD and HEAL those OPPRESSED BY THE DEVIL, you are going to DO GREATER WORKS and become the viable member of the church God desires us to be, but there are things that will kill the engine of the Holy Spirit entirely.

The number one, top-of-the-list DUNAMIS killer is your attitude.

Jesus went home and, on the sabbath day, entered the synagogue to teach, but instead of willing listeners, He faced a wall of disbelief.

"From whence hath this man these things? and what wisdom is this which is given unto him, that even such MIGHTY WORKS are wrought by his hands? Is not this the carpenter, the son of Mary, the brother of James, and Joses, and of Juda, and Simon? and are not his sisters here with us? AND THEY WERE OFFENDED AT HIM."

"But Jesus said unto them, A prophet is not without honour, but in his own country, and among his own kin, and in his own house. AND HE COULD THERE DO NO MIGHTY WORK, save that he laid his hands upon a few sick folk, and

healed them. And he marvelled because of their UNBELIEF." (Mark 6:2-6)

"Mighty works" in both verses 2 and 5 is the word DUNAMIS. Notice, the people knew Jesus did mighty works, but Jesus COULDN'T DO mighty works among them. Why? Because they'd taken OFFENSE. Also notice, Jesus called that UNBELIEF.

Being offended by His ministry was the SAME THING as not believing in God's POWER in Him, and that killed the engine. It didn't matter that they KNEW HE COULD DO MIGHTY WORKS. They'd seen the lame walk and the blind see. He could do NOTHING but pray for a few sick folk. The word "few" there means "puny."[17] Their unbelief limited Him to a puny result.

Thayer's Greek Definitions defines "offended" as:

"To put a stumbling block or impediment in the way, upon which another may trip and fall; to cause a person to begin to distrust and desert one whom he ought to trust and obey; to see in another what I disapprove of and what hinders me from acknowledging his authority; to judge unfavourably or unjustly of another; one who stumbles or whose foot gets entangled [and] feels annoyed; to be displeased, indignant."

That covers a lot of territory. Doesn't it? The people who knew Jesus in His youth couldn't get past their memories of him as a kid and therefore didn't acknowledge His AUTHORITY. Although they heard it in His words, although they realized His wisdom when He spoke, they judged Him unjustly and stumbled.

---

[17] G3641

I love the visual image of "one whose foot gets entangled." Vincent's Word Studies furthers this mental picture. It defines "offended" from its use in Matthew 5:29. Here, Jesus said it was better to pluck out your eye if it offends you than to fall into hell through any sin it causes. The commentary says:

"The stick in a trap on which the bait is placed, and which springs up and shuts the trap at the touch of an animal. Hence, generally, a snare, a stumbling-block."

Ah, that wily devil! He's set a trap for you, dangling his shiny bait in your path.

"You don't like that person, do you?" he whispers in your ear. "Remember what they did to you?" Or perhaps, he has you speculating on the person's motive. They are probably being selfish and leaving you out. You swallow it, hook, line, and sinker, without even talking to them!

Blindly, we walk right into the snare, caught by our offended mindset.

Jesus COULD NOT DO MIGHTY WORKS there, the DUNAMIS that He was ANOINTED with to HEAL and DELIVER those OPPRESSED BY THE DEVIL was ineffective in the face of their OFFENDED mindset.

And here's an important thing to know – This means taking OFFENSE at anything or anyone. **Your attitude toward people in your daily life will affect what the Holy Spirit can do through you**, and if the devil can catch you in his trap, if he can make you angry at someone and full of unforgiveness, then he can stop the power of God from fully working in the church.

It doesn't matter if you believe in miracles, Christians full of OFFENSE will not experience them in their midst.

A preacher demonstrated a visual analogy about the

belief in tithing. He climbed a ladder onstage and threatened to hurl himself from the top. "I've decided today not to believe in gravity," he said. This seems like ludicrous behavior. We believe in gravity 100%. But his point was effectively made. Whether or not you believe in tithing, it is a principle in God's Word.

So is the effect of OFFENSE on the miracles the church desires to see.

The disciple, Peter, called Jesus the *"Rock of offense,"* which causes people to stumble,[18] and Jesus said He'd come to set son against father, daughter against mother, daughter-in-law against mother-in-law.[19] No truer prophecy has been spoken.

What we've failed to connect on that is the consequences of it, yet they are throughout God's Word. Offense always keeps God's children from the blessings He desires to give.

The Israelites

The Israelites complained about manna from heaven. They were tired of it.

Here, God had given them a supernatural sign of His abundance and care, but they whined for the cucumbers, garlic and onions they'd had when they were slaves in Egypt.[20]

"At least, we had fish," they cried.

Needless to say, Moses *and* God were both displeased by their attitude.[21] Moses made a rather passionate prayer, demanding help to care for them, and

---

[18] 1Pe 2:8 AMPC
[19] Mt 10:35
[20] Num 11:5-6
[21] Num 15:10

God gave instructions to select 70 elders to dedicate to this task. He then made the Israelites a fateful promise.[22]

"And say thou unto the people, Sanctify yourselves against to morrow, and ye shall eat flesh: for ye have wept in the ears of the LORD, saying, Who shall give us flesh to eat? for it was well with us in Egypt: therefore the LORD will give you flesh, and ye shall eat. Ye shall not eat one day, nor two days, nor five days, neither ten days, nor twenty days; But even a whole month, until it come out at your nostrils, and it be loathsome unto you: because that YE HAVE DESPISED the LORD which is among you, and have wept before him, saying, Why came we forth out of Egypt?" (Numbers 11:18-20)

They despised the Lord with their attitude. How grave that is. They despised His deliverance. They despised His provision BY COMPLAINING.

Moses went out from God's presence and repeated to them all that God had said. He set up elders to help govern the people, as he'd been directed, and it says the Spirit of the Lord fell on the elders and they prophesied until dark.

God showed up in an incredible manifestation.[23]

The children of Israel witnessed it. They heard the elders' prophetic words. They knew they'd displeased God, and I would think repentance would be their next reaction. Instead, when God's words about an abundance of flesh to eat came true, they were gluttonous and paid for it with their lives.

---

[22] Num 11:11-17

[23] Num 11:25-26

"And there went forth a wind from the LORD, and brought quails from the sea, and let them fall by the camp, as it were a day's journey on this side, and as it were a day's journey on the other side, round about the camp, and as it were two cubits high upon the face of the earth. And the people stood up all that day, and all that night, and all the next day, and they gathered the quails: he that gathered least gathered ten homers: and they spread them all abroad for themselves round about the camp. And while the flesh was yet between their teeth, ere it was chewed, the wrath of the LORD was kindled against the people, and the LORD smote the people with a very great plague." (Numbers 11:31-33)

I figured it up using a search engine. A man can walk approximately 20 miles in a day. Using simple math, 20 miles by 20 miles is 400 square miles. Converting things further, 2 cubits is 3 feet. So that means, 400 square miles of quail 3 feet deep! Now consider, they gathered each man, at least, 10 homers. One homer is 58 liquid gallons. That means each man had 580 gallons of quail.

Those are approximate figures, but how sobering. Plus, it says the people died while eating. That suggests something about the quail wasn't fit to eat. Maybe *ecoli*. Who's to say?

But it was their COMPLAINTS that caused the whole thing.

Now, I don't want you to get sidetracked thinking God made them sick. God is GOOD all the time. Don't fall into the devil's trap and think otherwise. The plague was the result of the Israelites behavior, and they had ample warning of it and plenty of time to change their attitude. God had done miraculous incredible things for them that they treated as worthless.

Hebrews 10:26-31 says:

"Now if we willfully persist in sin AFTER RECEIVING SUCH KNOWLEDGE OF THE TRUTH, then there is no sacrifice left for those sins— only the fearful prospect of judgment and a fierce fire that will consume God's adversaries. Remember that those who depart from the law of Moses are put to death without mercy based on the testimony of two or three witnesses. Just think how much more severe the punishment will be for those who have turned their backs on the Son of God, trampled on the blood of the covenant by which He made them holy, and outraged the Spirit of grace WITH THEIR CONTEMPT. For we know the God who said, "Vengeance belongs to Me—I will repay," also said, "The Eternal One will judge His people." It is truly a frightening thing to be on the wrong side of the living God." (VOICE)

Though this talks about the extreme end of persistent UNBELIEF, the point is effectively made.

The GOOD NEWS is that God is a God of mercy and forgiveness, and any man who approaches Him with a humble heart, transparent in what he's said or done wrong ... and God knows of it anyway, I would point out ... that man or woman will receive complete redemption and all of God's grace.

This is God's heart, to FORGIVE.

Peter asked Jesus how many times he should forgive his brother, and Jesus replied, *"Seventy times seven."*[24] What God has asked man to do, He always does in an even greater measure. He is a God of peace, a place of sanctuary and safety. He is faithful and kind and gentle.

He is also holy and asks our obedience to His

---

[24] Mt 18:21-22

principles. If we want to be BOLD in our faith and STRETCH FORTH a hand to HEAL, then we must watch our words.[25] Our negative words will kill the engine of faith required to take us forward into being the disciples God desires in His church.

[25] Act 4:29-30

Chapter 7

The Critical Church

The apostle Paul remonstrated with the Galatian church for falling back on the procedures in the Mosaic law.

"O foolish Galatians, who hath bewitched you, that ye should not obey the truth ...?" he asked. *"Received ye the Spirit by the works of the law, or by the hearing of faith? Are ye so foolish? having begun in the Spirit, are ye now made perfect by the flesh?"* (Galatians 3:1-3)

Now, fast-forward to chapter 5. Here, Paul says:

"For in Jesus Christ neither circumcision availeth any thing, nor uncircumcision; BUT FAITH WHICH WORKETH BY LOVE." (Galatians 5:6)

Faith is the key to the engine. Only through the use of faith is God pleased.[1] Not because of grandiose sermons, nor advanced college degrees. Not because of total dollars we've given. In fact, nothing we do on our own energy will please God. Only faith.

And faith works through love.

Remember Mark 11:24-26 that we read earlier?

"Therefore I say unto you, What things soever ye desire, when ye pray, believe that ye receive them, and ye shall have them. AND WHEN YE STAND PRAYING, FORGIVE, if ye have ought against any: that your Father also which is

---

[1] Heb 11:6

in heaven may forgive you your trespasses. But if ye do not forgive, neither will your Father which is in heaven forgive your trespasses." (Mark 11:24-26)

FORGIVENESS is the outgrowth of love. It is love exercised. We must have faith for effective prayer, but we cannot pray and expect God to answer with unforgiveness between us and a brother or sister in Christ.

Remember also, 1 Corinthians 13:2.

"And though I have all faith, so that i could remove mountains, and have not charity, I AM NOTHING."

If we are not living a life of love with our neighbor, then our prayers will not work. **With OFFENSE in our hearts, the DUNAMIS of the Holy Spirit, the NATURE OF GOD, His Resurrection POWER to perform SIGNS and WONDERS to us and through us is completely cut off.**

Faith is the key that cranks the engine, but the spark needed is fueled by love.

Or let me put it this way. God IS love, and nothing outside of LOVE can come into His presence. OFFENSE and UNBELIEF, hate and strife, are works of darkness. Love and hate will never, ever mix.

The Warning about Offense

John the Baptist was thrown into prison, and it seems, his time there filled him full of doubt because he sent two of his disciples to ask Jesus if He really was the expected Messiah.

Jesus answer seems at odds with itself at first.

"Jesus answered and said unto them, Go and shew

John again those things WHICH YE DO HEAR AND SEE: The blind receive their sight, and the lame walk, the lepers are cleansed, and the deaf hear, the dead are raised up, and the poor have the gospel preached to them. And blessed is he, WHOSOEVER SHALL NOT BE OFFENDED IN ME." (Matthew 11:4-6)

We get the first part. Jesus points out the miracles that He'd performed. Surely, those were proof enough. But He didn't stop there, He also warned against OFFENSE.

If we keep reading, Jesus then defends John to the surrounding crowd. This says so much to me about Jesus' love for him. But at the end of his speech, Jesus makes an analogy that refers back to his earlier remark.

"Why is it that when John came to you, neither feasting nor drinking wine, you said, 'He has a demon in him!'? Yet when the Son of Man came and went to feasts and drank wine, you said, 'Look at this Man! He is nothing but a glutton and a drunkard! He spends all his time with tax collectors and other affluent sinners.' But God's wisdom will be visibly seen living in those who embrace it.'" (Matthew 11:19-20 TPT)

They were offended by John's abstinent ways. They were offended by Jesus' feasting. It didn't matter which side He walked on, they refused to believe. In the following verses, this becomes even more clear. Jesus calls out the towns by name that had witnessed His miracles and turned their backs.[2] How sobering.

We can see this warning again in Luke 17:1, where Jesus says, *"It is impossible that no offenses should come."*

---

[2] Mt 11:20-24

Some translations state this as *"no occasions for stumbling."*

There will always be opportunities to take offense, our reaction to those opportunities is what makes the difference. Do we commit our thoughts and emotions to what upset us, or will we walk with God and let it go?

I have practiced letting go a lot in recent years. It started with not yelling at drivers. This seems laughable really, but I could not drive anywhere without blowing up at someone and reacting badly. I finally saw myself when the driver I had gotten so upset with knew me and mentioned it to my daughter.

Let me tell you, that will sober you quick. From then on, I made a determined effort to not take offense. I'd catch myself grumbling again ... someone had cut me off ... but I'd take a deep breath and release it. Then I'd apologize to God. I'd pray a blessing on that person.

I also learned to "let go" at home. My husband likes to cook, but I am a bit of a control freak in the kitchen. I was sure he needed my advice! One day, I tried and tried to instruct him, and we ended up in an argument instead.

At that moment, I had the biggest revelation – I didn't have to stand there while he cooked. I could walk away! I let go after that. Now, I take my younger dog and go for a walk outside. I am at peace. My husband is at peace. And in peace, there is great strength.

A peaceful man is a self-controlled one. He isn't weakened by his emotions or prey to the devil's trap of offense. He stands strong in the ANOINTED ONE with the shield of FAITH in his hand and PEACE on his feet.[3]

That is how we should walk.

Criticism only births more criticism. This is a spiritual principle. The words we speak create what we desire,

---

[3] Eph 6:15-16

whether it's positive or negative. And often it is both at once. The book of James compares it to a drinking fountain that spills both good water and undrinkable water.[4] If we talk badly about someone else, then we not only remove the ability of our FAITH to work, we will step outside of God's will for us. People we could have helped won't get our help, AND something we value, that we've worked so hard on, will be crucified by someone else.

Jesus said:

"Don't pick on people, jump on their failures, criticize their faults— unless, of course, you want the same treatment. That critical spirit has a way of boomeranging." (Matthew 7:1 MSG)

I also like The Passion Translation of this verse: *"Refuse to be a critic full of bias toward others, and judgment will not be passed on you."*

Don't be a critic. About her hair. Or his shirt. Or that Evelyn is in the choir but can't sing. Or that Joe mutters when he talks. Or that your neighbor doesn't mow his grass. Or that his kids are unruly. Or that Jill lost her job and you know it was through critical mistakes.

Let me make this clear. **YOU ARE NEVER ALLOWED TO BE CRITICAL OF ANYONE EVER.**

The scribes and Pharisees dragged a woman in front of Jesus, having caught her in an adulterous affair. They thought to trap him and embarrass her. Yet, Jesus didn't say anything at all. In fact, He acted like He didn't hear them.[5]

When they continued to pester Him, He finally stood and spoke one sentence. *"He that is without sin among you,*

---

[4] Jas 3:10-11

[5] Jn 8:3-6

let him first cast a stone at her."[6]

He knelt again and went back to drawing in the dirt.

Let's be clear again: She WAS an adulteress. She WAS full of sin. But He REFUSED to criticize her.

He had GOOD to do, people to HEAL, demons to CAST OUT. He had to be SINLESS to die on the cross and become the sacrifice for the entire world. He could not afford to SPEAK in OFFENSE, either to her for who she was or to the Pharisees and scribes for their behavior.

We need to learn from that and bite our tongue.

Thieves and Robbers

Jesus healed a man born blind, and the people who knew the man questioned him about how he'd been healed. This drew the attention of the Pharisees.[7] The Pharisees questioned the healed man later, then unsatisfied with his answers, called for his parents. The man's parents assured the religious leaders their son had always been blind, careful to phrase their answer to avoid referring to Christ. This would get them kicked out of the synagogue for sure.[8]

The Pharisees called for their son again and barraged him with more questions. "Who healed you? What exactly did he do?"

Exasperated with them, the formerly blind man said, "Look. I was blind. Now I can see. Only a man from God could do a miracle like this."[9]

Enraged, they kicked him out of the synagogue. FOR EXPERIENCING A MIRACLE.

Pay attention, church! They knew he was born blind.

---

[6] Jn 8:7

[7] Jn 9:6-8, 13

[8] Jn 9:18-22

[9] Jn 9:30-33

They could see he'd been healed. They clearly knew Jesus was involved. But they were angry and OFFENDED.

Now, it touches me that when Jesus heard about the man's troubles, He found him and reassured him about who He was. He was concerned for the man's soul.[10]

But I want to read Jesus' words to the Pharisees afterward.

"Verily, verily, I say unto you, He that entereth not by the door into the sheepfold, but climbeth up some other way, THE SAME IS A THIEF AND A ROBBER." (John 10:1)

Now skip down a few verses.

"Then said Jesus unto them again, Verily, verily, I say unto you, I am the door of the sheep. ALL THAT EVER CAME BEFORE ME ARE THIEVES AND ROBBERS: BUT THE SHEEP DID NOT HEAR THEM. I am the door: by me if any man enter in, he shall be saved, and shall go in and out, and find pasture. THE THIEF COMETH NOT, BUT FOR TO STEAL, AND TO KILL, AND TO DESTROY: I am come that they might have life, and that they might have it more abundantly." (John 10:7-10)

Notice the words "thieves and robbers."

When the Holy Spirit spoke these verses to my heart, **He said the thieves (plural) and robbers (plural) are often our neighbor, our co-worker, or that person that we don't get along with.** They are PEOPLE. We expect the thief to be the devil in a red costume with horns and a pitchfork, so we're not prepared when he turns out to be someone we know, someone we've met, or even a complete stranger who crosses our path.

---

[10] Jn 9:35

In this story, the thieves and robbers WERE THE CHURCH. That *is* who Jesus spoke to. He wanted the Pharisees to know they scattered the sheep with their OFFENDED mindset. He wanted them to know they were acting like the devil![11]

What a sober thought that is. The church, meant to be a place of healing, had become, instead, a DEN OF THIEVES,[12] and OFFENSE was how the wolf entered and destroyed the sheep.[13] Both by spreading strife amongst its members and because their words prevented faith from doing any MIGHTY WORKS.

A church without the POWER OF GOD in manifestation, a church that cannot DO GOOD, is no church at all, and remember a church is the people not the building.

How can we, so called followers of the ANOINTED ONE, show up on Sunday and cut someone down who sits across the aisle? Or who doesn't go to church? Or who doesn't go to OUR church? Or who isn't in our denomination? Or who is not of our culture? Or who is the wrong gender to be ministering?

But wait. You feel justified in that because the Bible says ...

No, stop right there! The Bible SAYS there is no male or female, Jew or Greek, for all ARE ONE in Christ.[14] The Bible SAYS Christ died for WHOSOEVER, not just men and not just women.[15] The Bible SAYS the unbelieving husband can be saved by the wife's behavior, and the unbelieving wife can be saved by the husband's behavior. The

---

[11] Jn 10:13
[12] Mt 21:13
[13] Jn 10:12
[14] Rm 10:12; 1Co 12:13; Gal 3:28
[15] Jn 3:16; Rm 10:13

ANOINTING of Christ can work through both.[16]

The Bible says, *"And it shall come to pass in the last days, saith God, I will pour out of my Spirit upon ALL FLESH: and YOUR SONS AND YOUR DAUGHTERS SHALL PROPHESY, and your young men shall see visions, and your old men shall dream dreams: And ON MY SERVANTS AND ON MY HANDMAIDENS I will pour out in those days of my Spirit; and they shall prophesy."*[17]

The Bible SAYS through the apostle Paul that we are to do whatever we can to save the lost.

"For though I be free from all men, yet have I made MYSELF SERVANT UNTO ALL, that I might gain the more. And unto the Jews I became as a Jew, that I might gain the Jews; to them that are under the law, as under the law, that I might gain them that are under the law; To them that are without law, as without law, (being not without law to God, but under the law to Christ,) that I might gain them that are without law. To the weak became I as weak, that I might gain the weak: I AM MADE ALL THINGS TO ALL MEN, THAT I MIGHT BY ALL MEANS SAVE SOME." (1 Corinthians 9:19-22)

Paul even goes so far as to say not to condemn someone (through our behavior) who disagrees with what we're eating. If you eat something dedicated to an idol in front of someone who is weak in their beliefs about that and it causes them to stumble, then you have done incorrectly.

"Wherefore, if meat make my brother to offend, I will eat no flesh while the world standeth, lest I make my brother to offend." (1 Corinthians 8:13)

---

[16] 1Co 7:14

[17] Act 2:17-18

The Voice Translations states it this way: *"So if any type of food is an issue that causes my brothers and sisters to fall away from God, then God forbid I should ever eat it again so that I would NEVER BE THE CRACK, THE RISE, or THE ROCK ON THE ROAD that CAUSES THEM TO STUMBLE."*

NEVER BE THE CRACK IN THE ROAD that causes someone to STUMBLE.

You can't get any clearer than that. The world is looking at you every day when you go into the marketplace. Do you act like Christ? Do you make them want to know Him? Or do you drive them away?

What picture do you paint of the people in the church?

Chapter 8

The Submissive Church

A friend of mine led me to a book on marriage that, at first glance, hit me like a punch in the gut. The title alone was sobering, but I felt to read it, and I'm so glad I did! It dealt a lot with how to overcome anger, a definite issue I've had. It also had a great deal of Scripture on the power of submission.

Now, I want to go in deeper detail on the different sides of offense, so that you can fully see it. But that book got me thinking about submission, and in studying to write this book, I had a revelation.

Let's reread a statement the apostle Paul made in 1 Corinthians 9.

"For though I be free from all men, yet have I made MYSELF SERVANT UNTO ALL, that I might gain the more." (1 Corinthians 9:19)

Paul an apostle of God, a man with great revelation of the Scriptures, a man called to the Gentiles, a controversial thing at the time, this man of faith who would write the majority of the New Testament submitted himself to the people, more concerned for their hearts than his personal glory.

In this, He imitated Christ.

Jesus knelt and washed the disciples' feet, and Peter, as usual, tried to prevent it. Jesus corrected him, twice nonetheless, then made a powerful statement.

"If I then, your Lord and Master, have washed your

feet; YE ALSO OUGHT TO WASH ONE ANOTHER'S FEET. For I have given you an example, that YE SHOULD DO AS I HAVE DONE to you. Verily, verily, I say unto you, The servant is not greater than his lord; neither he that is sent greater than he that sent him." (John 13:14-16)

Did you hear that? **We are to submit TO ONE ANOTHER.**

Much is made of a wife submitting to her husband; I referred to these verses in an earlier chapter. But if you read them with the Holy Spirit as instructor, you see the husband is a tender servant to his wife and submissive to his colleagues and to the people in the church and to the pastor and … to EVERYONE.

"And to the husbands, you are to demonstrate love for your wives WITH THE SAME TENDER DEVOTION THAT CHRIST DEMONSTRATED TO US, HIS BRIDE … All that he does in us is designed to make us a mature church for his pleasure, until we become A SOURCE OF PRAISE TO HIM—glorious and radiant, beautiful and holy, without fault or flaw … Marriage is the beautiful design of the Almighty, a great and sacred mystery—meant to be A VIVID EXAMPLE OF CHRIST AND HIS CHURCH. So every married man should be gracious to his wife just as he is gracious to himself. And every wife should be tenderly devoted to her husband." (Ephesians 5:25, 27, 32-33 TPT)

How beautiful that is phrased. Submission is to make the church A SOURCE OF PRAISE to God, a glorious, beautiful, radiant, holy example of who He is. Our submission is CLEANSING for the soul. This holy image is what we are meant to project, and submission to each other is the way it happens.

This seems impossible. Being honest, sometimes, even among Christians, certain people rub me the wrong way. There's a statement I heard in the past which helps me with this – In the body of Christ, of which we are all members, the nose doesn't have to associate with the armpit.

This is humorous, but my point is, you must BE submissive and ACT loving, you must guard your words, but you don't have to spend intimate time together. People have different personalities that sometimes don't fit well. And besides, there is an element of submission that we have overlooked, one key to our success at it.

The Scripture says in James 4:7:

"SUBMIT YOURSELVES THEREFORE TO GOD. Resist the devil, and he will flee from you."

We believe this 100%. In order to resist the devil, we must first submit ourselves to God. We commit to that. Our hands raised in prayer, we lay our lives at God's feet, saying we'll work on being kind to others. We'll work on submitting to our boss, who is difficult to work for. We'll pray over being submissive to our mother-in-law.

The problem with that mentality is we hold them as two separate things. We think we can be submitted to God OR submitted to a person. If we succeed with one, well, at least, that's halfway.

No! Think of 1 Corinthians 13:1-3 again. Remember? Faith without love does nothing. Now think of Galatians 5:6. Faith only works by love. Also include Mark 11:24-25 where it says, when you are praying, forgive your brother first.

These are the behaviors of submission.

If you hate your brother or sister, if you are critical of them, if you are OFFENDED by them, if you think you know better and, by George, they're going to find out how they ought to do things ... then YOU ARE NOT SUBMITTED TO GOD AT ALL.

Any behavior outside of God's love and forgiveness takes you out of SUBMISSION TO GOD and walks you away from faith. If I choose to speak badly about the driver who cut me off, I'm not submitted to God. If I talk about the minister on TV because he has a large church, I'm not submitted to God. If I grumble because the waitress doesn't treat me as well as someone else, I'M NOT SUBMITTED TO GOD.

Because submission to God walks in *agape* love with everyone. How does Ephesians describe the husband's care for his wife?

"Husbands have the obligation of LOVING AND CARING for their wives the same way they love and care for their own bodies, for to love your wife is to love your own self. No one abuses his own body, but pampers it—serving and satisfying its needs. That's exactly what Christ does for his church!" (Ephesians 5:28-29 TPT)

The wife is to submit to her husband, but the husband is a loving, caring person just as Christ was a servant to his disciples, as He washed their feet and gave His life for them. A husband is to reflect Christ in that same measure.

What an example to us, the church!

"Let this mind be in you, which was also in Christ Jesus: Who, being in the form of God, thought it not robbery to be equal with God: But made himself of no reputation, and TOOK UPON HIM THE FORM OF A SERVANT, and was made in the likeness of men: And being found in fashion as a

man, HE HUMBLED HIMSELF, and became obedient unto death, even the death of the cross." (Philippians 2:5-8)

Christ became a servant, a man of humility. Not weak. The fact He resisted sin so completely tells us that. But in His obedience to death, He was far stronger than we can ever know.

We are called to this same level of submission, with one huge difference. Christ's victorious Resurrection has given us the Holy Spirit's help.

1 Peter 5:5 says:

"Likewise, ye younger, SUBMIT YOURSELVES unto the elder. Yea, ALL OF YOU BE SUBJECT ONE TO ANOTHER, and be clothed with humility: for God resisteth the proud, and GIVETH GRACE TO THE HUMBLE."

Only through humility in a behavior of SUBMISSION can we partake of God's grace and reflect the loving heart of God to a hurting, dying world in need of our magnificent Savior. He is our example, but He is also the POWER to do it.

A Church of Hypocrites

We read much of the Scriptures as a story without applying the words to ourselves. We say it was for the Israelites in that time or spoken to the people, who didn't understand what was happening. But EVERY WORD *"is profitable for doctrine, for reproof, for correction, for instruction in righteousness."*[1]

The Passion Translation says it this way: *"It will empower you by its instruction and correction, giving you the strength to take the right direction and lead you deeper*

---

[1] 2Ti 3:16

into the path of godliness."

In the Voice Translation we can see this passage even clearer.

"In its inspired voice, we hear useful teaching, rebuke, correction, instruction, and training for a life that is right."

These words of life spoken through men by the Holy Spirit are to stop us in our tracks when we are doing the wrong thing. They are to correct us and show us what is godly and how to walk better. Hebrews 12:9 compares this correction to that of an earthly Father. If our earthly dad corrected our childish behavior, how much more should our heavenly Father?

But just like a child can choose to continue to disobey, we have to make up our minds to receive the correction and determine, with God's help, to stop what we are doing and act differently. The apostle Paul referred to this as discipline and compared it to an athlete running a race for a prize. I like the Passion Translation which refers to it as self-control, which you should recall is a fruit of the Spirit listed in Galatians.[2]

Reading back in Hebrews 12, verse 11 further enlightens us on this.

"Now all discipline seems to be more pain than pleasure at the time, yet later it will produce a transformation of character, bringing a harvest of righteousness and peace to those WHO YIELD to it." (TPT)

A harvest of RIGHTEOUSNESS AND PEACE. This is

[2] 2Co 9:25; Gal 5:22-23

what we want. But that requires changing our thoughts and zipping our lips. We YIELD and let God deal with other people's mistakes and, thereby, concentrate on our own. This was the most freeing realization to me. I don't have to be the judge. I don't have to "fix them," but can turn them over to God and go on with my day joyfully.

No amount of our criticisms changes the other person anyway. Instead, it increases strife, which remember, the Scripture says is the source of confusion and "EVERY EVIL WORK."[3] Ouch. It is that serious to watch our words.

Strife is a "work of the flesh" listed with witchcraft, hatred, and heresy, amongst other sins.[4] **It is anti-God and promotes discord and disunity. It also separates you from what the Holy Spirit would work in you.**

To walk in the Spirit, we must crucify, or put to death, our fleshly nature.[5]

It is one or the other. We will listen to our fleshly mind and indulge hatred and strife, or we will promote peace. We will speak life through the Holy Spirit and DO GOOD or we will sow seeds of destruction. Proverbs 11:9 refers to the latter-type man as a hypocrite.

"An hypocrite with his mouth destroyeth his neighbor."

Webster's Dictionary of American English (1828) defines "hypocrite" as: "One who feigns to be what he is not; one who has the form of godliness without the power, or who assumes an appearance of piety and virtue, when he is destitute of true religion."

Thayer's Greek Definitions says in the New

---

[3] Jas 3:16

[4] Gal 5:20-21

[5] Gal 5:24-25

Testament it means "an actor, stage player."[6] This should open our eyes wide.

Jesus used the word a number of times when talking to the Pharisees, RULERS IN THE CHURCH. The most powerful instance is found in Matthew 23. It must be said, first, that Jesus was meek, or gentle, in nature, but that did NOT make him weak. He'd come, remember, to bring correction. He *is* the Word.[7]

He said to the people, *"So listen and follow what they teach, but don't do what they do, for they tell you one thing and do another ... Everything they do is done for show and to be noticed by others. They want to be seen as holy."*[8]

He goes on to say the Pharisees need for show was arrogant and ungodly. They desired the best seat at the banquet. They worked to look pious. They even tried to appear like they were converting lost souls. But all of it was a sham because inside they were dead men.

I want us to see one particular statement here. Remember, these were religious leaders, and lest you think the words don't apply to you, you're just a congregation member, after all ... rewind and reread the purpose of the Scriptures. This is for our correction. It helps us walk in righteousness.

In Matthew 23:23, Jesus says:

"You ignore the most important duty of all: to walk in the love of God, to display mercy to others, and to LIVE WITH INTEGRITY."

"Integrity" is defined as "wholeness, unbroken state; the entire, unimpaired state of a thing, particularly of the

---

[6] G5273

[7] Jn 1:1

[8] Mt 23:3, 5 TPT

mind, moral soundness or purity, uprightness, honesty ... genuine, as integrity of language."[9]

It is how your act and how you talk, and it evidences itself in you as the love of God and mercy to others. It is purity of thought and speech. You are honest but kind. In other words, you WALK IN THE SPIRIT and NOT in the flesh.

Anything else make us a hypocrite, no better than the Pharisees, who appeared religious but were not. God forbid, anyone could say this of THE CHURCH.

Jesus said to them, *"Outwardly you masquerade AS RIGHTEOUS people, but inside your hearts you are FULL OF HYPOCRISY and lawlessness."*[10]

God forbid we sit in the pew, raise our hands in worship, or take notes on the sermon, then turn around and criticize Sister Sarah because she went on a cruise. Or because Brother Jones took our parking spot. Or someone new sat in our seat.

"But the wisdom that is from above is first pure, then PEACEABLE, gentle, and easy to be intreated, full of mercy and good fruits, without partiality, and WITHOUT HYPOCRISY. And the FRUIT OF RIGHTEOUSNESS IS SOWN IN PEACE of them that make peace." (James 3:17-18)

Are you making peace? Is the wisdom of God in you EASY for others to see? Is it WITHOUT PARTIALITY? Does someone hear your words and know they are truthful? And by that, I don't mean blunt and rude. **We are to speak gentle words OR NOTHING AT ALL. If it doesn't SOW PEACE, then DON'T SAY IT.**

Read what the book of James says again:

---

[9] Webster's, 1828

[10] Mt 23:28 TPT

"We all fail in many areas, but ESPECIALLY WITH OUR WORDS ... We use our tongue to praise God our Father and then TURN AROUND AND CURSE A PERSON who was made in his very image! Out of the same mouth we pour out words of praise one minute and curses the next. My brothers and sister, this should never be!" (James 3:2, 9-10 TPT)

Now add in Paul's words from Ephesians.

"Therefore, as a witness of the Lord, I insist on this: that you no longer walk in the outsiders' ways—with minds devoted to WORTHLESS pursuits ... But this is not the path of the Anointed One, which you have learned ... So PUT AWAY YOUR LIES and speak the truth to one another because we are all part of one another. When you are angry, don't let it carry you into sin. Don't let the sun set with anger in your heart OR GIVE THE DEVIL ROOM TO WORK. ... Don't let EVEN ONE ROTTEN WORD SEEP OUT OF YOUR MOUTHS. Instead, offer only fresh words THAT BUILD OTHERS UP when they need it most. That way your good words will COMMUNICATE GRACE to those who hear them." (Ephesians 3:17, 20, 25-27, 29 VOICE)

In the midst of this passage about our speech, he says, *"It's time to stop bringing grief to God's Holy Spirit."*[11]

Oh, Lord, forgive us for our worthless talk. Forgive your people of their lies and for causing strife. Forgive us for the hatred we've shown to others both in and out of the CHURCH. Forgive us for giving the devil room to work, for tearing down instead of building up.

Forgive us for grieving your Holy Spirit and destroying the GOOD we are called to do. For trafficking in

[11] Eph 3:30 VOICE

the OPPRESSION OF THE DEVIL instead of STRETCHING FORTH YOUR HAND TO HEAL.

Because that is the consequences of our HYPOCRISY, and this is not how we learned to be like Christ.

What Offends Me

There will always be opinions to deal with. Ours. Other people's. Other Christians'. The secular world's. And every man and woman will believe what they think is right.

Proverbs 16:2 gives this additional meaning.

"We are all IN LOVE WITH OUR OWN OPINIONS, convinced they're correct. But the Lord is in the midst of us, testing and probing our every MOTIVE." (Proverbs 16:2 TPT)

Opinions are not TRUTH, and opinions will always have the wrong motive. They are selfish and self-centered. TRUTH only comes through Jesus Christ,[12] and anything outside of Him is doomed to failure.

Especially the methods of the ever-changing secular world. We should not share their opinions.

"STOP IMITATING THE IDEALS AND OPINIONS OF THE CULTURE AROUND YOU, but be inwardly transformed by the Holy Spirit through a TOTAL REFORMATION OF HOW YOU THINK. This will EMPOWER you to discern God's will as you live a beautiful life, satisfying and perfect in his eyes." (Romans 12:2 TPT)

Stop trying to be like them.

God alone knows the heart,[13] and His desire is for

---

[12] Jn 14:6

[13] Ps 44:21

our thoughts to mirror His, not the world or the culture or any ideals made by men. **We will have a beautiful, satisfying life only when our minds are transformed to see things from God's perspective.**

He is TRUTH, and the opposite of TRUTH is unreliability, instability, and lies, and know that the devil is the father of lies.[14] Opinions are fickle. They come and go like shadows during the day. One minute, they appear one way and another they've changed.

God would have us depend on Him instead.

"Trust in the Lord completely, and DO NOT RELY ON YOUR OWN OPINIONS. With all your heart rely on him to guide you, and he will lead you in every decision you make." (Proverbs 3:5 TPT)

Only in Christ is there any faithfulness.[15] He is the ROCK, a figure of stability, that the CHURCH was built upon because He is reliable, sure, and steady.[16]

He is wise, whereas our opinions are foolish.[17] They go against God's wisdom, requiring actions that are outside of the straight and narrow path.[18] It's much easier to walk on the broad way that leads to destruction, easier to give into our opinions and let them sway us.[19]

"A fool is in love with his own opinion, but wisdom means being teachable," it says in Proverbs 12:15.[20] And later in Proverbs 18:2: *"A [self-confident] fool has no delight in understanding but only in revealing his personal opinions*

---

[14] Jn 8:44
[15] 1Co 1:9; Rev 1:5
[16] Mt 16:18
[17] 1Co 1:30
[18] Mt 7:14
[19] Mt 7:13
[20] TPT

and himself."[21] He doesn't have to know what he's talking about. He's just proud that he spoke.

It doesn't matter what I think, what you think, what some newsman thinks, or a politician, or even the pastor of your church. An opinion is always faulty. And loud. Whereas a man of humbleness keeps his thoughts silent, knowing the damage they can cause, a fool makes sure everyone hears him.

Jesus spoke about His people as lights in the darkness. He said we are to be open to His words and not hardhearted and consumed with our own.[22] Because we can be misled by our thoughts.

Our mind says we are afraid, but that is a lie. Our mind says our feelings are hurt, but God bids us to love and forgive.

"Open your heart and consider my words. WATCH OUT THAT YOU DO NOT MISTAKE YOUR OPINIONS for revelation-light!" (Luke 11:35 TPT)

Don't confuse your thoughts with God's.

I hate watermelon. My parents love it. These are opinions. I am not a fan of sports of any kind. My aunt loves sports. These are also opinions. We understand this plainly, but when someone says an opinion within the church about how services should run, for instance, we go a little blind.

The many denominations came into being largely for this reason. People could not get their opinions to agree on an infinite number of small things within the church.

News flash. OPINIONS WON'T AGREE. EVER. Opinions are hypocritical. They require of others what the

---

[21] AMPC

[22] Lk 11:34

speaker does not fully do himself.

"How could you say to your friend, 'Let me show you where you're wrong,' when you're guilty of even more? You're being hypercritical and a hypocrite!" (Matthew 7:4-5 TPT)

Opinions are fraudulent. They are the very essence of pride and arrogance, saying, "Do what I say because I said it!" They require a behavior without setting an example. Or while thinking we are setting an example when, in fact, we aren't.

They take away our reliance on God and place it on the flesh.

"An arrogant man is inflated with pride— nothing but a snooty scoffer IN LOVE WITH HIS OWN OPINION." (Proverbs 21:24 TPT)

"There's only one thing worse than a fool, and that's the smug, conceited man ALWAYS IN LOVE WITH HIS OWN OPINIONS." (Proverbs 26:14 TPT)

Opinions do not promote the love of God for our neighbor, which the Word says should be as high, as great as our love for ourselves![23] I want the best for me. I should also want the best for you. But usually, through our opinions, we are not thinking of our neighbor's needs, only of our own. Opinions are absent of mercy and devoid of God's grace. They divide and break apart.

"Rumors and opinions about the true identity of Jesus

---

[23] Mt 19:19

DIVIDED THE CROWD." (John 7:43 VOICE)

Your opinion, my opinion, his opinion is the last thing we should EVER take as gold. Instead, we seek only God's ways on an issue. **We obey His instructions and stay united as the *living* church.**

"Live in harmony with each other. Don't become snobbish but take a real interest in ordinary people. Don't BECOME SET in your own opinions." (Romans 12:16 PHILLIPS)

I love the Passion Translation of the previous verse: *"Live happily together in A SPIRIT OF HARMONY, and be AS MINDFUL OF ANOTHER'S WORTH AS YOU ARE YOUR OWN. Don't live with a lofty mind-set, thinking you are too important to serve others, but be willing to do menial tasks and identify with those who are humble minded. Don't be smug or even think for a moment that you know it all."*

Opinions promote strife, and this is a dangerous thing. They call godly what is ungodly. They justify themselves as correct and righteous, and they are not dependent on God.

"But those who call the work of God the work of Satan UTTERLY REMOVE THEMSELVES FROM GOD," it says in Matthew 12:32[24]

What does God want to do through you that He can't because you're too hung up on what you think? And know this, it doesn't have to be related to the issue at hand. Your spiteful words about your husband will keep the Holy Spirit from using you IN ANY AREA.

We cannot say we profess to be of God while acting

---

24 VOICE

like the devil.

"And so the good man (who is filled with goodness) speaks good words, while the evil man (who is filled with evil) speaks evil words. I tell you this: on the day of judgment, people will be called to account FOR EVERY CARELESS WORD they have ever said." (Matthew 12:35-36 VOICE)

We must seek first the kingdom of God. How do we do that? By cherishing every word of the Scriptures. By putting into use what we've been told. We are to love our neighbor, regardless of who he is or how he acts, and that means, to put it bluntly, SHUTTING UP.

There is no Scripture anywhere that allows you to judge anyone. On the contrary, the Bible is overflowing with instruction about kindness and compassion.

"BANISH bitterness, rage and anger, shouting and slander, and ANY AND ALL MALICIOUS THOUGHTS—these are poison. INSTEAD, be kind and compassionate. Graciously forgive one another just as God has forgiven you through the Anointed, our Liberating King." (Ephesians 4:31-32 VOICE)

Here is the power of the Word of God. That when I catch myself speaking words I shouldn't say, I stop and repent, apologize, if necessary, and say something different. I must do this EVERY TIME. God EMPOWERS ME to do this, and I promise if this becomes a regular practice, your thoughts will change.

This is how we "pull down strong holds" in our mind. It is the purpose for our spiritual weapons. We use them AGAINST the devil's words IN US, anything He tries to use to prevent the KNOWLEDGE OF GOD from entering.

"(For the weapons of our warfare are not carnal, but mighty through God to the pulling down of strong holds;) CASTING DOWN IMAGINATIONS, and every high thing that exalteth itself against the knowledge of God, and BRINGING INTO CAPTIVITY EVERY THOUGHT to the obedience of Christ." (2 Corinthians 10:5)

YOUR MIND and YOUR THOUGHTS will change and YOUR ACTIONS as a result. Not that the issue which upset you will dissolve and become any different, but that it no longer affects you. You will have JOY in the midst of seemingly difficult situations. This is God's will for His children. This is why His JOY gives us strength.[25]

God's joy is a spiritual weapon wielded against all forms of hate. It keeps us in line with His will and His ways, and then the Holy Spirit can use us to DO GOOD and draw others to Christ. We can speak words of HEALING. We can ENCOURAGE those having a bad day.

But our opinions are harmful EVERY TIME. They draw people away from the gospel. Instead of DOING GOOD, we DO HARM.

In Romans 14, the apostle Paul has strong words about this.

"It's high time that you welcome all people weak in the faith WITHOUT DEBATING AND DISPUTING THEIR OPINIONS ... We must resolve NEVER TO JUDGE others and NEVER TO PLACE AN OBSTACLE OR IMPEDIMENT IN THEIR PATHS that could cause them to trip and fall." (Romans 14:1, 13 VOICE)

How sobering. Our words can destroy and condemn

[25] Neh 8:10

or lift and encourage. We can turn others TOWARD CHRIST and welcome them into the CHURCH, or we can send them running where they'll never come back.

God, help us to never do that.

Chapter 9

The Silent Church

The book of James has much to say about walking by faith as it affects our behavior. In the first chapter, James talks about faith and patience, about being doubtful in our minds, and about the source of temptation – our lusts.[1]

In verses 19-20, he gives specific instructions about our words of anger.

"Wherefore, my beloved brethren, let every man be swift to hear, slow to speak, slow to wrath: For the WRATH OF MAN WORKETH NOT THE RIGHTEOUSNESS OF GOD." (James 1:19-20)

Our anger does no one any good. It cannot work righteousness. This is so clear.

James goes on to say having liberty in God requires "bridling," or restraining,[2] our tongue. Otherwise, we are DECEIVED, and remember the devil is the DECEIVER, and our religion is in vain, or worthless.[3]

When we turn to chapter 2, he starts off with an analogy about our opinions.

"My dear brothers and sisters, how can you claim to have faith in our glorious Lord Jesus Christ if you favor some people over others? ... If you give special attention and a good seat to the rich person, but you say to the poor one,

---

[1]Jas 1:3, 6, 14

[2] G5468

[3] Jas 1:26

"You can stand over there, or else sit on the floor"—well, doesn't this discrimination show that your judgments are guided by evil motives?" (James 2:1, 3 NLT)

Wealth or lack of wealth is not a reason to choose one person over another. In fact, if we do that, we have EVIL MOTIVES.

We could dwell here for a while. This also applies to other areas of our opinions. We cannot favor people because of gender, culture, skin color, IQ, education, denomination, and the list goes on. However, James isn't done with the topic.

In chapter 3, which we read in part already, we find a lengthy discussion on the power of the tongue, which is called a *"fire of hell," "iniquity," "deadly poison,"* and *"cursing."*[4] Then he goes on to introduce strife. Strife is a *"lie against the truth," "earthly, sensual, devilish," "confusion," "every evil work,"* and *"hypocrisy."*[5]

Three strong chapters abundant in truth.

But I want to pause on the beginning of chapter 4.

"From whence come WARS AND FIGHTINGS among you? come they not hence, even of your lusts that war in your members? Ye lust, and have not: ye kill, and desire to have, and cannot obtain: ye fight and war, yet ye have not, because ye ask not. Ye ask, and receive not, because YE ASK AMISS, THAT YE MAY CONSUME IT UPON YOUR LUSTS." (James 4:1-3)

It is plain that we cannot say anything we want to say, that our thoughts on most any matter are wrong and

---

[4] Jas 3:6, 18, 10

[5] Jas 3:14-17

ungodly. I cannot leave you there, though, with no way to fight what WILL HAPPEN in your minds. What do you do if someone hurts you and it's real and awful and they *were* wrong? What then?

Let's reread James 4:3.

"When you pray for things, you don't get them because you want them for the wrong reason—for your own pleasure." (GW)

This statement comes after three chapters about what we say and how we act, that we are tempted by our lusts and full of strife and envy. That these attitudes cause dissension and death. We pray, it says here, solely for our own pleasure.

Now, this isn't necessarily talking about acquiring physical things, praying for a boat or a car. The topic here is *"wars and fightings."* The word "fightings" means "controversy," which I find very apt.[6]

1 Peter 2:11 puts the thought this way:

"Dearly beloved, I beseech you as strangers and pilgrims, abstain from fleshly lusts, which WAR AGAINST THE SOUL."

Our lusts cause battles amongst each other; our strife about controversies destroys our soul. We pray for our own pleasure something that sounds more like, "God, run him into a light pole." This isn't a prayer at all but is selfish and demonic.[7] It is FOR OUR OWN PLEASURE.

In James 4:11, the author gives strong words against

---

[6] G3163
[7] Jas 3:15

this kind of speech. "Don't set yourself up as a judge," he says. Notice, it does not qualify this with, "When he is right, and you are wrong." No, it's we NEVER judge one another because life is short and wishing evil on someone else is a sin.[8]

"Therefore to him that KNOWETH TO DO GOOD, AND DOETH IT NOT, to him IT IS SIN." (James 4:17)

We've missed the importance of this verse. DOING GOOD to someone in the face of what they probably did wrong is a huge part of Christianity. Yes, they said that, and they meant it at the time. Yes, they hurt you. But you are still to DO GOOD.

Revenge belongs to God.[9] **When we are injured by someone, instead of taking revenge, we lay the issue at God's feet and refuse to speak evil.** James 5:16 encourages us toward repentance and prayer for each other instead.

But also, let's read the apostle Paul's instructions in Romans 12.

"Therefore if thine enemy hunger, feed him; if he thirst, give him drink: for in so doing thou shalt heap coals of fire on his head. Be not OVERCOME OF EVIL, but OVERCOME EVIL WITH GOOD." (Romans 12:20-21)

Giving into the desire to hate lets the devil OVERCOME you. DOING GOOD, on the other hand, defeats him every time.

Trust me. I know how hard that is to swallow. I am telling you nothing I have not worked out in myself, and let

---

[8] Jas 4:14

[9] Rm 12:19; Heb 10:30

me reassure you, with practice, it is possible to do. I started by NOT SPEAKING EVIL. Sometimes, the best GOOD I could DO was being SILENT and walking away. I'd give myself time to cool down and think clearly again, time to pray over how to behave.

I'm very open with the Lord. I'd say something like, "God, she hurt my feelings a lot, and being honest, I want to clobber her. I don't know what to do with all this anger."

Eventually, I'd add, "Bless her with wisdom and peace today."

Because her being a nicer, better person will prevent our problem with each other from repeating itself. The truth is, no one knows what that person is going through. Someone who hurts others needs more of Jesus, not less.

My mom helped me with this thought pattern immensely. She always says that you cannot wish a curse on someone. For example, "I hope they go broke and have to move." God will not answer that kind of prayer. But, "God give him a better job that promotes him where he can live somewhere nicer," is entirely possible. God answers spoken blessings.

Matthew 7:12 increases this idea. It says:

"In EVERYTHING you do, be careful to treat others IN THE SAME WAY YOU'D WANT THEM TO TREAT YOU, for that is the essence of all the teachings of the Law and the Prophets." (Matthew 7:12 TPT)

Not simply DO GOOD and SPEAK BLESSINGS but also treat them how YOU WANT TO BE TREATED. This thought takes the fire out of my anger every time. I don't want someone to be mad at me. I don't want to be yelled at or spat on or maybe simply ignored. I don't want hateful things done to my home or my daughter or my dogs. What I wish on them, if I think about it happening to me, I let the anger go!

If anything, on a bad day when my head hurts and my car won't crank and my dog threw up on the rug and my husband is testy because of problems at work, I want someone to pat me on the back and buy me a donut.

I realize doing that for some people is impossible, but your attitude, your heart, is what God is looking at. Are you going to step in the TRAP of OFFENSE or are you going to bypass it and CHOOSE JOY?

Two verses in 1 Peter speak of this attitude loudly to me. 1 Peter 2:20 states:

"For what glory is it, if, when ye be buffeted for your faults, ye shall take it patiently? but if, when YE DO WELL, AND SUFFER FOR IT, ye take it patiently, this is acceptable with God." (1 Peter 2:20)

Let's also read it in the New Living Translation: *"Of course, you get no credit for being patient if you are beaten for doing wrong. But IF YOU SUFFER FOR DOING GOOD AND ENDURE IT PATIENTLY, God is pleased with you."*

Not reacting in anger, not taking revenge, is definitely suffering. Especially if you know you were right. This happens within marriage all the time. But we must ask ourselves if being right is more important than being at peace. I can assure you it isn't.

Remember, God is the judge of the heart. He knows what they were thinking and why. It is His job to correct them, not ours. Ours is to SEEK PEACE, to PURSUE IT.[10] Something we are pursuing, we will chase after to obtain. When my world fell apart, I wanted peace more than

[10] Ps 34:14; 1Pe 3:11

anything else. I had to face my anger along with my fears and get rid of both. I ran to obtain PEACE, whatever it required of me to have it.

1 Peter 3:17 is another powerful verse.

"For it is better, if the will of God be so, that YE SUFFER FOR WELL DOING, than for evil doing."

It's better to suffer in the flesh, knowing you are DOING GOOD and CHOOSING PEACE than to suffer because you said what you shouldn't have. This is godly suffering. Not that God puts us into evil circumstances, so we learn something, but that our reaction to OFFENSE and UNGODLINESS isn't always going to be comfortable.

The Bible is our manual. The Holy Spirit is our teacher. Jesus is our example of a Christian life. A good God who does good things will never do anything that isn't good.[11] Not sickness and disease or heartache or any other form of destruction. OPPRESSION is of the devil. Instead, we suffer as Jesus did, who heard what was said about Him and died for those people anyway.

These are the words of Hebrews.

"For consider him that endured such contradiction of sinners against himself, LEST YE BE WEARIED AND FAINT IN YOUR MINDS. Ye have not yet resisted unto blood, striving against sin." (Hebrews 12:3-4)

I don't have to fight sin. Jesus did that for me. He sent the Holy Spirit and DUNAMIS to guide me through life. I can be STRONG in the Lord, OVERCOME EVIL, and DO GOOD. I can become the true CHURCH, as God wants it to

---

[11] Rm 12:21; Jas :17

be. I can share the HEALING POWER of God's message and do the GREATER WORKS He desires. The Word of God promises that is the method toward a beautiful, fruitful life.[12] But it requires me to decide to do it.

Being peaceful in the face of offense is a position of great power. Being submissive to others when they have wronged us is strength. The devil has fooled us into thinking otherwise. For one thing, being peaceful keeps us connected to God and the POWER of HIS NATURE. Being in a right relationship with Him is crucial to victory.

One man in the Bible understood this well.

David

The most many of us know of David is he defeated Goliath with a slingshot and eventually became king. We may read his psalms and find comfort in them but have no idea why he wrote them. Why all the talk about being persecuted that seems so prevalent?

To fully understand, we must first talk about King Saul.

The nation of Israel wanted a king. This was not God's desire. He wanted to be their Source. They wanted a fallible icon. They wanted to be like all the ungodly nations around them.[13] This is worth taking a moment to think about. After all God had done for them, the GREAT SIGNS and WONDERS He'd performed in Egypt, the dividing of the waters of the Red Sea, they rejected Him to look like the heathen world. Like idol worshippers.[14]

God gave into their wishes, though not without stern

---

[12] Jas 3:13 TPT
[13] 1Sa 8:5, 7, 19-20
[14] 1Sa 10:19

warning, and He chose Saul.[15]

Saul had great success initially against their enemies. He defeated the Ammonites.[16] He won a key battle against the Philistines, through his son.[17] But facing another, stronger Philistine army, and the growing fear of the people, he disobeyed the Mosaic law and, without waiting for the prophet Samuel to arrive, offered the pre-battle sacrifice himself.[18]

When Samuel found out, the consequences were severe.

"And Samuel said, What hast thou done? And Saul said, Because I saw that the people were scattered from me, and that thou camest not within the days appointed, and that the Philistines gathered themselves together at Michmash; Therefore said I, The Philistines will come down now upon me to Gilgal, and I have not made supplication unto the LORD: I forced myself therefore, and offered a burnt offering. And Samuel said to Saul, Thou hast done foolishly: thou hast not kept the commandment of the LORD thy God, which he commanded thee: for now would the LORD have established thy kingdom upon Israel for ever. BUT NOW THY KINGDOM SHALL NOT CONTINUE: the LORD hath sought him A MAN AFTER HIS OWN HEART, and the LORD hath commanded him to be captain over his people, because thou hast not kept that which the LORD commanded thee." (1 Samuel 13:11-14)

Saul allowed fear to overwhelm him, instead of relying on God.

---

[15] 1Sa 9:17; 1Sa 10:1

[16] 1Sa 11:11

[17] 1Sa 13:3

[18] 1Sa 13:9

He made excuses, largely blaming the people, but in God's eyes, the damage was done. God removed him from the kingship forever and sought A MAN AFTER HIS OWN HEART.[19]

A moving description. To understand it, though, we must look closer at His choice of David.

It is interesting to know that the prophet Samuel was reluctant to let go of Saul. When he's standing in Jesse's house prepared to anoint the new king, a familiar scene to us, he's come because God told him to stop mourning Saul.[20] He watched Saul continue to disobey and has spoken strong words to him. In one instance, Saul was told to kill the Amalekites and to destroy their goods, but Saul allowed the people to take the spoils of battle, and he kept the king alive. This displeased God so much that Samuel killed the king himself![21]

You can imagine, then, the emotion behind the aged prophet seeking someone else and thinking David's brother, Eliab, was an excellent choice. He's there reluctantly, his emotions clouding his judgment; he's afraid of Saul's reaction and has come in secrecy.[22] Now, God tells him Eliab is not the one.

"But the LORD said unto Samuel, Look not on his countenance, or on the height of his stature; because I have refused him: for the LORD seeth not as man seeth; for man looketh on the outward appearance, BUT THE LORD LOOKETH ON THE HEART." (1 Samuel 16:7)

What did God see in David to make such a fantastic

[19] Act 13:22
[20] 1Sa 16:1
[21] 1Sa 14:24; 1Sa 15:18-21, 33)
[22] 1Sa 16:2

statement that even the prophet did not understand it? Fast forward to David taking a stand against Goliath, and we'll get a glimpse.

The Scriptures tell us that David was not unknown to Saul. When David was anointed king in the presence of his brothers, the Holy Spirit left Saul and an evil spirit started tormenting him. Seeking mental solace, Saul asked for a man to play music which would comfort him.

His servants suggested David.

"Then answered one of the servants, and said, Behold, I have seen a son of Jesse the Bethlehemite, that is cunning in playing, and a mighty valiant man, and a man of war, and prudent in matters, and a comely person, and the LORD is with him." (1 Samuel 16:18)

That's quite a description. David was a talented musician and an attractive youth. He's described as "mighty" and "valiant," meaning he was a strong warrior,[23] and he was also "prudent." This is a word meaning "to distinguish, understand," to be "eloquent."[24] In other words, he was well-spoken and smart.

Most importantly, Saul's servants had heard of David, so apparently David had quite a reputation already. They knew that God was with him, and I have to think if the servants of Saul knew all this, then David's brothers weren't deaf and blind either. Probably, it played into his brother's scolding comments when he inquired about killing Goliath.

"And Eliab his eldest brother heard when he [David] spake unto the men; and Eliab's anger was kindled against

---

[23] H1368, H3448

[24] H995

David, and he said, Why camest thou down hither? and with whom hast thou left those few sheep in the wilderness? I know thy pride, and the naughtiness of thine heart; for thou art come down that thou mightest see the battle." (1 Samuel 17:28)

Eliab was Samuel's first choice for king and got passed over, remember? For his kid brother, nonetheless. Everyone's talking about David, and he's a little sore.

What were they saying, though? What had a young shepherd boy done that was so notable?

Well, look at David's own words. All his questions about killing Goliath brought him before Saul again.

"And David said unto Saul, Thy servant kept his father's sheep, and there came a lion, and a bear, and took a lamb out of the flock: And I went out after him, and smote him, and delivered it out of his mouth: and when he arose against me, I caught him by his beard, and smote him, and slew him. THY SERVANT SLEW BOTH THE LION AND THE BEAR: AND THIS UNCIRCUMCISED PHILISTINE SHALL BE AS ONE OF THEM, SEEING HE HATH DEFIED THE ARMIES OF THE LIVING GOD. David said moreover, The LORD that delivered me out of the paw of the lion, and out of the paw of the bear, he will deliver me out of the hand of this Philistine. And Saul said unto David, Go, and the LORD be with thee." (1 Samuel 17:36-37)

David had been noticed for killing a lion and a bear, for protecting his father's sheep! He had placed his strength in God to aid him in their deliverance, and people acknowledged it.

The servants said, "The Lord is with him."

David credited those victories to God. God had

delivered him, and God received the glory for those mighty acts.

David understood covenant. To keep it simple, this is God's unbreakable promise, sworn in blood. David called Goliath "uncircumcised." Circumcision was a sign of the blessing of God on the nation of Israel. It was part of their covenant obedience that went back to the blessing on Abraham.[25] David knew what God had promised His people and called upon it to defeat his enemies.

Israel had a covenant with God. The Philistines didn't.

We know how the story goes. Goliath taunted David, making fun of his age and his good looks. No way someone so pretty would defeat him. Without mighty weapons, nonetheless.[26] But David laid his entire confidence in God.

"Then said David to the Philistine, Thou comest to me with a sword, and with a spear, and with a shield: but I COME TO THEE IN THE NAME OF THE LORD OF HOSTS, the God of the armies of Israel, whom thou hast defied. This day will the LORD deliver thee into mine hand; and I will smite thee, and take thine head from thee; and I will give the carcases of the host of the Philistines this day unto the fowls of the air, and to the wild beasts of the earth; THAT ALL THE EARTH MAY KNOW THAT THERE IS A GOD IN ISRAEL. And all this assembly shall know that THE LORD SAVETH NOT WITH SWORD AND SPEAR: for the battle is the LORD'S, and he will give you into our hands." (1 Samuel 17:45-47)

Not words of defiance, but words of FAITH. "I come in the name of THE LORD ... This day will THE LORD deliver

---

[25] Ge 17:11
[26] 1Sa 17:42

thee into my hand … that the entire earth WILL KNOW THE GOD OF ISRAEL."

Words after God's own heart. Not "I will," but "God will."

If you read through the life of David, this is always his behavior. He prayed over every battle before he entered it and waited for an answer from God on whether he should go to war or not. With one exception, the death of Bathsheba's husband, David's murderous sin. Know, though, that Solomon was his son by her, and Solomon went on to be king, over all his brothers, which were many. And Solomon wasn't the oldest son nor should he have been God's first choice.[27]

God's forgiveness is grand. It is wide and deep. And His love for David, who placed God first, would make David the lineage of the Savior of the world.

David vs. Saul

David's story is largely one of him running from Saul. Every victory God gave David reminded the king, yet again, of how he'd disobeyed and of God's rending the kingdom from him. Add in the evil spirit which tormented him, and the words of David's psalms make a lot more sense. But notice in them his dependence on God as well, how despite his troubled circumstances he always placed his safety in God's capable and willing hands.

David hid from Saul continually, outsmarting the king's many attempts to kill him. I want to look at one such instance because it fits into this book.

In 1 Samuel 24, we have David hiding in a cave. Keep in mind this is not their first encounter of this nature. Plus, King Saul knew David would succeed him. This means, upon

[27] 2Sa 5:14;1 Ki 1:17, 43

his death, David will reign as king. The Bible tells us Saul heard David's praises sung in the land. The people loved David.[28]

Let's pick up the story in the New Living Translation.

"After Saul returned from fighting the Philistines, he was told that David had gone into the wilderness of En-gedi. So Saul chose 3,000 elite troops from all Israel and went to search for David and his men near the rocks of the wild goats. At the place where the road passes some sheepfolds, Saul went into a cave to relieve himself. But as it happened, David and his men were hiding farther back in that very cave! 'Now's your opportunity!' David's men whispered to him. 'Today the Lord is telling you, 'I will certainly put your enemy into your power, to do with as you wish.' So David crept forward and cut off a piece of the hem of Saul's robe." (1 Samuel 24:1-7)

Here, we see a pivotal moment. Saul has chosen to enter the cave for a menial reason, and it happens to be the same cave that David is hiding in. He's completely unaware David is there.

As we said, David knows he will be king when Saul dies, so here's an opportunity to advance things and relieve the continual threat of death. Saul has tried to kill him numerous times. Why not take advantage of the situation? Surely, God is behind such an amazing coincidence.

David entertains the idea, for a moment. He creeps forward. But instead of killing him, he opts to cut off a piece of Saul's robe. We might think this makes him weak. But remember David is known for his victories in battle. He isn't weak.

---

[28] 1Sa 18:6-8, 16

Let's keep reading.

"But then David's conscience began bothering him because he had cut Saul's robe. He said to his men, 'THE LORD FORBID THAT I SHOULD DO THIS TO MY LORD THE KING. I shouldn't attack THE LORD'S ANOINTED ONE, for the LORD HIMSELF HAS CHOSEN HIM.' So David restrained his men and did not let them kill Saul." (1 Samuel 24:6-7)

Wait. What? Why would David say that? Who cares if Saul is anointed! He's trying to kill him!

Don't stop reading yet.

"After Saul had left the cave and gone on his way, David came out and shouted after him, 'My lord the king!' And when Saul looked around, David bowed low before him. Then he shouted to Saul, 'Why do you listen to the people who say I am trying to harm you? This very day you can see with your own eyes it isn't true. For the Lord placed you at my mercy back there in the cave. Some of my men told me to kill you, but I spared you. For I said, 'I will never harm the king—HE IS THE LORD'S ANOINTED ONE.' Look, my father, at what I have in my hand. It is a piece of the hem of your robe! I cut it off, but I didn't kill you … MAY THE LORD JUDGE BETWEEN US. Perhaps THE LORD WILL PUNISH YOU for what you are trying to do to me, but I will never harm you …" (1 Samuel 24:9-12 NLT)

David understood an important principle. God is the judge, not man. His battles were won because God had delivered him. Revenge was man's way; King Saul's life belonged to God.

Why, though? What was David's motive for restraint? Here's the key we must see—**BECAUSE GOD HAD**

ANOINTED HIM.

"But I thought God took the kingdom away from him because of his sins," you say.

He did. That's a fact. But the OFFICE OF KING was anointed by God, and not even David, who had favor with God, had the right to rebel against it. His OPINION of Saul didn't matter. His fears for his life weren't greater than Saul's anointing as king.

Saul was full of sin and tormented by hate. He had only bad plans for David, and he would continue to chase him after this. But David knew he had no right to slander the man God had placed in authority.

So strong was his belief in this that after Saul and Jonathan were killed in battle, David made sure Israel mourned them properly.[29] Years later, he had their bones reburied in honor.[30] He hunted down the Amalekite responsible for their deaths and killed him for it.[31] He killed the man who killed Saul's son, Ishbosheth.[32] Then, in a promise he'd made to Saul, and because of a covenant he'd made with Saul's son, Jonathan, he sought out Jonathan's remaining heir, restored to him his father's lands and prosperity, and invited him to eat at the king's table for the remainder of his life.[33]

Would you and I go to such an extent for a declared enemy? Would we DO GOOD to that level for someone who hates us? Probably not. But David understood the damage that would be done by his OPINIONS. Even though they were justified, they were ungodly.

David chose SUBMISSION to the man God had

---

29 2Sam 1:4, 11-12, 17-18

30 2Sa 21:13-14

31 2Sa 1:14-16

32 2Sa 4:10-12

33 2Sa 9:9-11

anointed. Despite Saul's failings. Despite the danger to himself. Though he had more than one opportunity to end things in his favor, he didn't take any of them, and God honored him with a long, victorious life.

The power of silence

Search the Bible from front to back, pour through the psalms, study every word of David's life, and you will not find any instance where he spoke a curse against King Saul. You won't find any words of retribution. David even forbade his men from acting against Saul.[34]

We can say that he suffered well.

Jesus set us this example in a scene we've read many times but glossed over. Taken before Pilate and asked for a defense against the charges given by the Jews, He said nothing.

"And Pilate asked him again, saying, Answerest thou nothing? behold how many things they witness against thee. But Jesus yet answered nothing; so that Pilate marvelled." (Mar 15:4-5)

How did He do it? It wasn't through willpower or mental strength. It wasn't because He was the Word and had spoken the world into existence.[35] The ANOINTING on Him, the POWER of the Holy Spirit to PREACH the GOOD NEWS, the EXCELLENCE of God that caused people to hear His AUTHORITY and wonder at it, enabled Him, in that precarious moment, to keep silent.

1 Peter 2:22-23 clarifies this.

---

[34] 1Sa 24:7

[35] Jn 1:1-3

"Who [Jesus] did no sin, neither was guile found in his mouth: Who, when he was reviled, reviled not again; when he suffered, he threatened not; but COMMITTED HIMSELF TO HIM THAT JUDGETH RIGHTEOUSLY." (1 Peter 2:22-23)

"Guile" is "deceit" or a "trick." It can also mean "cunning."[36] In other words, Jesus didn't try to fool anyone with slick talk. We read this in the prophecy of Isaiah as well. Isaiah 53:9 says, *"Neither was any deceit in his mouth."* Jesus spoke no deceit. Never forget that the deceiver is the devil.[37]

Looking at 1 Peter 2:22-23 again, to be "reviled" means to be "reproached" or to "heap abuse" upon.[38] They spat on Him. They lied about Him. They called Him names. He didn't return it, though He'd once said He could pray, and His Father would send twelve legions of angels for His rescue.[39]

He suffered without making any threats. No words like, "Just you wait until I rise again!"

He didn't do any of those things but gave the power of His life to God to use and rescue, and in so doing, the Holy Spirit held Him silent.

Because Jesus knew the power of a word spoken in faith. He'd cursed the fig tree and watched it wither. Remember?[40] He knew one misspoken word, and everything He'd come to do … to die and take our sins, to defeat the devil, the OPPRESSOR of mankind, would be for nothing.

So great is the strength of our words. King Solomon said this in Ecclesiastes 5:6: *"Suffer not thy mouth to cause*

---

[36] G1388
[37] Rm 12:9
[38] G3058
[39] Mt 26:53
[40] Mk 11:14

thy flesh to sin." The Contemporary English Version states it this way: *"Don't let your mouth get you in trouble!"*

In Proverbs, he reiterated this, saying, *"Guard your words and you'll guard your life, but if you don't control your tongue, it will ruin everything."*[41] And again, *"Guard your words, mind what you say, and you will keep yourself out of trouble."*[42]

This is so very clear. Just as Jesus spoke to the fig tree and expected it to wither, every word we speak will bring results, either negative or positive. Jesus told us this in Matthew 12. He said what we say shows who we are. We either sound like Christians, people of THE ANOINTED ONE, or we sound like the devil, the DECEIVER.

Matthew 12:33 says, *"For the tree is known by his fruit."* An orange tree bears oranges, but also a HEALTHY orange tree bears HEALTHY fruit.[43]

Now, let's read in verse 37:

"For by thy words thou shalt be justified, and by thy words thou shalt be condemned."

Notice, our words JUDGE US righteous or JUDGE US guilty. **Our words against SOMEONE ELSE instead JUDGE US personally. They don't judge the other person at all.** This is sobering, and know this, it is regardless of whether our words about them are right or not.

How are we to react then when inside we are raging? Keep silent.

If Jesus through the Holy Spirit could keep silent in the face of His accusers, then we, through that same DUNAMIS, have the power to do the same.

---

41 Pr 13:13 TPT

42 Pr 21:23 VOICE

43 Jas 3:12

Chapter 10

The Praying Church

We are given specific instructions on how to deal with our enemies, and they aren't what you would think. We aren't to gossip about them, to warn others about them, to speak spitefully of them. We are to LOVE them. These are the words of Jesus.

"But I say unto you, LOVE your enemies, BLESS THEM that curse you, DO GOOD TO THEM that hate you, AND PRAY FOR THEM which despitefully use you, and persecute you; THAT YE MAY BE THE CHILDREN OF YOUR FATHER WHICH IS IN HEAVEN: for he maketh his sun to rise on the evil and on the good, and sendeth rain on the just and on the unjust." (Matthew 5:44-45)

They curse us, but we BLESS them. They use us, they take from us, our time, our goods, our pride, but we DO GOOD to them. Instead of being offended and criticizing, we PRAY for them. Only through these reactions will we look like our heavenly Father.

I want you to notice, EVERY PERSON who ever does or says anything unkind to you is included in this list. If they are an enemy, if they cursed you, if they hated you, if they used you and persecuted you, we are to LOVE them, BLESS them, DO GOOD, and PRAY for them.

Remember also we said, "Lord, run him into a light pole," is not God's idea of prayer.

We pray a BLESSING, and we refuse to SPEAK EVIL.[1]

---

[1] Jas 4:11

We don't indulge in slick talk to trick them into some trap we've laid. We speak no words of revenge, and we don't heap abuse upon them.

Jesus didn't do that, and we are told not to act like that.

"But the things that COME OUT OF YOUR MOUTH—your curses, your fears, your denunciations—these COME FROM YOUR HEART, and it is the stirrings of your heart that can make you unclean." (Matthew 15:18 VOICE)

In this passage, Jesus was teaching the multitudes on the real meaning of the law's commandments. To be unclean is to be defiled by sin. We are sinful because of what is in our heart. WHAT WE SAY paints a picture of what's inside us. When we say words of love and forgiveness, we reflect Christ. When we speak hate and strife, we look like darkness. There isn't any in between.

God's amazing grace, like David's protection of Jonathan's son, Saul's grandson, offered mercy and blessings we do not deserve. When we were the most vile, the most sinful, Jesus died for us, showing God's infinite love to the entire world.

David spoke mercy to his enemy, Saul. "I could have killed you, but I didn't because you are the king who God anointed."[2]

It says, King Saul wept hearing those words.

"And he said to David, Thou art more righteous than I: for thou hast REWARDED ME GOOD, whereas I have rewarded thee evil ... And now, behold, I know well that thou shalt surely be king, and that the kingdom of Israel shall be

---

[2] 1Sa 24:11

established in thine hand." (1 Samuel 24:17, 20)

How powerful! David's enemy praised his good deeds.

Christ didn't pick and choose who to die for. He gave His life for WHOSOEVER. All men, all cultures, all skin colors, all addictions, all fears. The rain from the sky falls on good people and bad ones.

This is our instruction. We are to speak GOOD to everyone, and speaking is part of DOING. We cannot hunger to DO GOOD, to HEAL those OPPRESSED OF THE DEVIL, we cannot pray to see God's divine POWER move and turn around and condemn anyone.

Ephesians 4:29 says this clearly.

"Let NO CORRUPT COMMUNICATION proceed out of your mouth, but that WHICH IS GOOD to the use of EDIFYING, that it may MINISTER GRACE unto the hearers."

Our words should edify and minister grace. Notice again, **there are no qualifications.** Not, they will only minister grace to good people, to people we like, or solely to our circle of friends. No, our words give grace TO THE HEARERS. Anyone listening. Or reading if it's something you say online. 99.9% of the time what I go to say in response to anyone on social media, I immediately delete.

The Holy Spirit in my ear, whispers, "You didn't need to say that."

He's right. I didn't. Not that we should appear weak to defend our faith. I want everyone to know I am a Christian. But that our defense should be stated with grace or not at all.

I like the God's Word translation of 1 Peter 3:15-16.

"But dedicate your lives to Christ as Lord. ALWAYS BE READY TO DEFEND YOUR CONFIDENCE IN GOD when anyone asks you to explain it. However, MAKE YOUR DEFENSE WITH GENTLENESS AND RESPECT. Keep your conscience clear. Then those who treat the good Christian life you live with contempt will feel ashamed that they have ridiculed you."

Just like King Saul saw God in David's behavior, that person who spoke against you will see God in yours. They may not admit it, and they don't have to admit it. We don't seek man's praises anyway. Our reaction is prayer, and if we can't pray right away, if we need time to overcome our anger and our need to strike out, then we sit silent or walk away. This is our ONLY allowed response.

The Importance of Prayer

The Holy Spirit gave me a depiction of prayer that increased its importance in my mind. I think we've belittled it somewhat. We pray during a church service, before meals, or at bedtime, and usually not anywhere else. We don't give it much weight.

Most of our idea of prayer is begging for something when we are desperate, but that makes prayer too small and insignificant. Prayer is our communication with God. It is how we spend time with Him and learn His character. It is also how we LISTEN to what He would say.

Prayer plays a part in the move of the Holy Spirit to DO GOOD and HEAL in the church.

I compared DUNAMIS to an engine, and unforgiveness, critical talk, and offense as pouring diesel fuel into an unleaded automobile's tank and destroying it. I said faith is the key that cranks the engine, love is the spark, and the Holy Spirit is the fuel. Well, there is one important element missing.

The Holy Spirit showed me a picture of myself seated in a car. I had a friend with me, and we were going somewhere I would go every day, meaning we weren't in a hurry or in an emergency. We were on the on ramp to the interstate with cars whizzing by at great speeds. Yet I couldn't find the gas pedal. I moved my seat forward twice, thinking I might reach it, but it was nowhere to be found.

I said to myself, "Maybe if I put the car in gear, it will roll forward, and I'll find it."

I did that, but it still wasn't there, so we went nowhere. Let me tell you, the stress of that moment. I had a car with nice seats. I had a friend with me who also wanted to go. I had an engine that worked and a tank full of fuel. I even had the keys and had cranked! But without a gas pedal, I was stuck!

Prayer is the effort we make to move the gas to the engine. It is the gas pedal. Without understanding prayer, we are on the lane of life, things hurling past us, unable to take hold or move out of the way to safety.

In the passage where Jesus threw out the moneychangers, He called the temple a "house of prayer." The moneychangers used it to steal from those who'd come to worship. This is the truth of the story. A minister pointed out that it wasn't simply that they were selling things there, but they were selling them dishonestly. This gives such meaning to Jesus' accusation.[3] People were harming people in a place meant for PRAYER to HELP people.

That is the bottom line of prayer, and the Bible gives it as our response to every circumstance and for any person, regardless of how they behave. We pray for those we love AND those we don't. We're told to pray for our enemies.

---

[3] Lk 19:46

We're told to pray for all men. We're told to pray for those in government.[4] This covers any human being anywhere, who lives and breathes.

Prayer is our ONLY choice. But even greater than that, it is the ONLY way to fuel the engine and move us forward in God's will for our success. We cannot expect anything of God and be unwilling to pray.

We must also know how to pray correctly.

The short book of Jude is mostly a warning against evil talk, boasting, and forms of ungodliness. It's interesting to read that it mentions murmuring and complaining alongside sexual sins and railing against the government. Then, it mentions prayer. It says:

"But ye, beloved, BUILDING UP YOURSELVES on your most holy faith, PRAYING IN THE HOLY GHOST, Keep yourselves IN THE LOVE OF GOD, looking for THE MERCY of our Lord Jesus Christ unto eternal life. And of some HAVE COMPASSION, MAKING A DIFFERENCE: And others save with fear, pulling them out of the fire; hating even the garment spotted by the flesh." (Jude 1:20-23)

Notice, prayer in the Holy Ghost builds us up in faith. It also keeps us walking in God's love toward others. Through prayer, we become merciful. We have compassion and can save those on the edge of hell. How serious prayer is!

Prayer is not simply, "God bless this food," but it is speaking in DUNAMIS that changes someone's life. It is connecting with God's NATURE, His MORAL CHARACTER, His INFLUENCE. Prayer changes them, and it changes us. I cannot pray and come away the same person.

---

[4] Mt 5:44-45; 1Ti 2:1-3

Romans 8 puts prayer into the realm of the spirit. It isn't simply physical words out of our minds, but **it comes from the guidance of the Holy Spirit, who knows what to say when we don't.** Holy Spirit prayer bypasses our minds and speaks mysteries to God.[5]

Romans 8:13-14 says:

"For if ye live after the flesh, ye shall die: but if ye THROUGH THE SPIRIT do mortify the deeds of the body, ye shall live. FOR AS MANY AS ARE LED BY THE SPIRIT OF GOD, they are the sons of God."

Notice, prayer requires "mortifying" or "putting to death" our fleshly reactions.[6] I like what Thayer's Greek Definitions says of this word "mortify." It says that "death [is] to be liberated from the bond of anything, literally to be made dead in relation to (something)."

We are dead to our criticisms, to offense and hate. We THROUGH THE HOLY SPIRIT'S POWER put all that away. Didn't we just talk about this this in Jesus' life, how He held silent in the face of His accusers? **The Holy Spirit can give you what to say in any situation, or He can empower you to say nothing at all.[7]**

Now let's read verses 25-26 of Romans 8:

"But if we wait expectantly for things we have never seen, then we HOPE WITH TRUE PERSEVERANCE and EAGER ANTICIPATION. A similar thing happens when we pray. We are weak and do not know how to pray, SO THE SPIRIT STEPS IN and articulates prayers for us with groaning too profound for words." (VOICE)

---

[5] 1Co 14:2
[6] G2289
[7] Lk 12:12

Prayer isn't of the flesh. It isn't spoken through what Jesus called "vain repetitions,"[8] but it comes from the spirit, or heart, of man. Prayer is Holy Spirit led and requires faith, or expectation, and it only brings results through an exercise of patience.

We anticipate God's answer. We persevere until we have it. Where we are weak, the Holy Spirit strengthens us for prayer. He is the go-between. He "aligns" our lives with the will of God and brings "good" and "beautiful" results.[9]

Through the Holy Spirit, our prayers are ANOINTED and FERVENT.

"Confess your faults one to another, and pray one for another, that ye may be healed. The EFFECTUAL FERVENT PRAYER of a righteous man availeth much." (James 5:16)

The phrase "effectual fervent" means "to put forth power."[10] We speak, not weak, ineffectual words, but POWERFUL ones that produce results.

Should we expect anything less of Holy-Spirit-led prayer? I think not! Fervent prayer, Holy Ghost prayer, will DO GOOD and HEAL those OPPRESSED OF THE DEVIL. It brings DUNAMIS onto the scene, moving us forward in the lane of life.

The apostle Paul said to run to obtain the prize.[11] The prize mentioned is the salvation of PEOPLE. We don't run for ourselves, but for the sake of the GOOD NEWS.[12] We run with patience, placing the desires of our flesh second to

---

[8] Mt 6:7
[9] Rm 8:27-28 VOICE
[10] G1754, Thayer's Greek Definitions
[11] 1Co 9:24
[12] 1Co 9:23

what the Holy Spirit desires.[13] We run for the salvation of others through fervent prayer and godly obedience.

We refuse offense. We submit ourselves to God and, through Him, to others. Our behavior and words look like and sound like Christ, which sometimes, means not saying anything at all. Where we are weak to do it, the Holy Spirit steps in to help.

We pray a BLESSING, not a curse, and to do that, to truly speak by faith over an enemy, there is one key element that cannot be missed.

Praise

"Rejoice evermore. Pray without ceasing. In every thing give thanks: for this is the will of God in Christ Jesus concerning you." (1 Thessalonians 5:16-18)

This is the instruction to the CHURCH. We are to rejoice. We are to pray without ceasing for all men, those we like and those we don't.[14] Additionally, we are to pray correctly. We cannot pray harm onto someone else. We are to speak blessing.

But the HOW TO DO IT escapes us. How do we pray for someone we don't like, who said horrible things about us or who did something heinous to us, and still be sincere before God? I struggled with this question for years. I handled it mostly by not praying at all. I figured better to say nothing than to say what I was thinking about that person.

However, notice these verses again. *"Pray without ceasing"* is sandwiched between *"rejoice evermore"* and *"in every thing give thanks."* This is significant.

Now, let's read Psalm 34:1.

---

[13] 1Co 9:26-27 TPT footnotes

[14] 1Ti 2:1-3

"I will bless the LORD AT ALL TIMES: his praise shall CONTINUALLY be in my mouth."

We *"pray without ceasing"* AND we *"praise continually."*

Prayer and praise are two halves of a whole. You cannot have true godly prayer without offering praise to God, and you cannot praise God without falling into prayer. We must be doing both ALL THE TIME.

When we do, praise will REPLACE our unkind, hateful words. Instead of fuming about the offense, whether it is legitimate or not, we PRAISE GOD. **Praise replaces what we would say with what we should say.** It's like flipping a light switch. If you turn the light on, then you are not in the dark.

We can see this principle in the parable of the sower as well. Where the cares of life would have us destroying the soil, instead of taking offense, which will PREVENT the POWER OF GOD from working, we choose to PRAISE and through praise to ROLL OUR CARES over onto God.

I like the Wycliffe Bible translation of this verse from 1 Peter.

"And cast ye all your busyness into him." (1 Peter 5:7 WYC)

What a great way to express it.

Other translations say, *"Pour out all your worries and stress,"* and *"You can throw the whole weight of your anxieties upon him."*[15] Stress, worry, anxiety, and busyness cover all the devil's work that we will face, all those things that cause us to say things we shouldn't.

Instead of voicing our fears, we thank God for His

---

15 TPT, PHILLIPS

protection.[16]

Instead of complaining about our spouse or coworker, we revel in God's love for us.

At each moment of the day, we choose PRAISE over frustration.

Returning to the illustration of a gardener again, we praise God through each point in the process. We praise Him for giving us the seed, although they still sit in our palm. We praise Him for the planting, knowing it will bear fruit. We praise Him while waiting for the seed to sprout. Waiting is a time of prayer and praise more than any other. It is PATIENCE instead of IMPATIENCE.[17]

We praise God when we see the plants sprout. What a miracle that is! We praise Him as they grow. Growth isn't always the most comfortable thing, but it's necessary to increase in the things of God.[18]

We praise as the fruit forms and REJOICE at the time of HARVEST for the amazing things God has done in us. All those months, we might have had to pull a few weeds, sit out a couple rainstorms, and sweat a little under the sun, but because our reaction was "Thank you, Jesus!" we had no room for complaints.

You will not complain about something you are praising God for, especially when the harvest has come.[19] And in that moment, we find another powerful truth. We PRAYED expecting God to answer. Then having been given the answer, holding God's abundance in our hands, we PRAISE HIM for it.

BUT He expects us to DO SOMETHING with it. The harvest is meant to be shared.

---

[16] Ps 91

[17] Ps 37:34, H6960

[18] Eph 4:15

[19] Mk 4:29

"And he [Jesus] spake a parable unto them, saying, The ground of a certain rich man brought forth plentifully: And he thought within himself, saying, What shall I do, because I have no room where to bestow my fruits? And he said, This will I do: I will pull down my barns, and build greater; and there will I bestow all my fruits and my goods. And I will say to my soul, Soul, thou hast much goods laid up for many years; take thine ease, eat, drink, and be merry. BUT GOD SAID UNTO HIM, Thou fool, this night thy soul shall be required of thee: then whose shall those things be, which thou hast provided? SO IS HE THAT LAYETH UP TREASURE FOR HIMSELF, AND IS NOT RICH TOWARD GOD." (Luke 12:16-21)

We are meant to GO INTO ALL THE WORLD and PREACH the GOOD NEWS, not sit in the pew with our treasure stuffed in the barn. The treasure isn't only for us.

Don't misunderstand. We are not meant to travel barefoot and hungry. God wants our needs provided for. He is the God of abundance. He is more than we can ever contain.[20] Jesus never missed a meal, out of poverty. He never went without proper clothing because He couldn't find two coins to purchase it. He told the seventy that went out that they would be provided for in their journey.

"And in the same house remain, eating and drinking such things as they give: for the labourer is worthy of his hire." (Luke 10:7)

But their purpose in GOING was to SHARE the HARVEST.[21]

---

[20] Ex 34:6; Eph 3:20
[21] Lk 10:2

Praise God for what He can do *for* me, but praise Him even greater for what He can do *through* me. Let these words I write be His words. Let Him receive the glory for their truth and for any understanding they give to others.

Though my fingers typed the keys, His heart spoke each thought, and I knew His voice because He is so very, very precious to me. I will GO, Lord, whatever the cost, and I know you will walk with me.

"A Psalm of David. Bless the LORD, O my soul: and all that is within me, bless his holy name. Bless the LORD, O my soul, and forget not all his BENEFITS: Who FORGIVETH all thine iniquities; who HEALETH all thy diseases; Who REDEEMETH thy life from destruction; who CROWNETH thee with lovingkindness and tender mercies; Who SATISFIETH thy mouth with GOOD THINGS; so that thy youth is renewed like the eagle's." (Psalms 103:1-5)

Chapter 11

The Rebellious Church

I somehow found myself on a Twitter thread, unsure what I'd clicked on to take me there. You know how that is. However it happened, a group of so-called "Christians" were railing against an issue in the church. I read in amazement the WORDS they spoke and couldn't help but think they'd wandered away from the TRUTH, both in the subject at hand and in their comments.

At another time, one of God's children said some things against the government that were filled with bitterness and unforgiveness going back many generations. I couldn't help but marvel at what I witnessed.

How has the CHURCH strayed so far from God's Word?

There is no qualification on forgiveness. Nowhere does it say you don't have to forgive *if* and then we're given a list of exceptions. With David as our example of how to behave, just as he treated King Saul with great respect (a man who sought to kill him), we must show respect for the office of the leaders placed over us in order to operate in the Holy Spirit in any measure.

And while you shake your heads at me, I didn't say that, Jesus did.

Now, let me point out that "government" means any sort of leadership from national to state to local law enforcement. It includes judges, your office manager, your pastor, your neighbor's pastor, and any selected leader of a group that you participate in. It is THE OFFICE of a person with designated authority over a group of people, no matter how large or small, and it is regardless of WHO is in that position, what political party they are a member of, their clean or unclean heart, any mistakes they've made, and any policies they've put into effect.

Remember, we are not the judge of the heart. We are not responsible for their choices only our REACTIONS to their choices. This includes voting, which is a form of speech (and our God-given responsibility) and any criticisms we have about the person holding that office. It includes TAKING OFFENSE against them. Like forgiveness, there is no exception allowed for being offended. Nowhere does the Bible say, "Don't be offended, except when it comes to leaders you dislike."

In fact, it says **RESISTANCE TO THE OFFICE OF AUTHORITY is like resisting God.** We read this in Romans 13:1-2.

*"Let every soul be subject unto the HIGHER POWERS [**any form of leadership**]. For there is no power but of God: THE POWERS THAT BE ARE ORDAINED OF GOD. Whosoever therefore RESISTETH THE POWER, RESISTETH THE ORDINANCE OF GOD: and they that resist shall receive to themselves damnation."*

Let's also read this in the Voice Translation and include the verses which follow.

"It is important that all of us SUBMIT to the authorities who have charge over us because GOD ESTABLISHES ALL AUTHORITY IN HEAVEN AND ON THE EARTH. Therefore, a person who rebels against authority rebels against the order He established, and people like that can expect to face certain judgment. You see, if you do the right thing, you have nothing to be worried about from the rulers; but if you do what you know is wrong, the rulers will

make sure you pay a price. Would you not rather live with a clear conscience than always have to be looking over your shoulder? Then keep doing what you know to be good and right, and they will publicly honor you ... SO SUBMISSION IS NOT OPTIONAL; IT'S REQUIRED. But don't just submit for the sake of avoiding punishment; SUBMIT AND ABIDE BY THE LAWS BECAUSE YOUR CONSCIENCE LEADS YOU TO DO THE RIGHT THING. Pay your taxes for the same reason because the authorities are servants of God, giving their full attention to take care of these things. Pay all of them what you owe. If you owe taxes, then pay. If you owe fees, then pay. In the same way, GIVE HONOR AND RESPECT TO THOSE WHO DESERVE IT." (Romans 13:1-7)

"Those who deserve it" means those IN THAT OFFICE deserve our respect. It isn't a loophole to include your opinion of them. There is no "way out" of this SUBMISSION. Submission to the office is like submitting to God, and remember, if we hold hate or offense for a person, then we aren't submitted to God.

As if that's not quite enough, read the next verse.

"Don't owe anyone anything, with the exception of LOVE TO ONE ANOTHER—that is a debt which never ends—because the person who loves others has fulfilled the law." (Romans 13:8 VOICE)

Here is submission to authority and love for one another spoken in the same thought! **Our submission to a governmental office shows our love for God.** We cannot expect to fulfill God's Word and act outside of His love.

Paul had more of a reason to dislike authority than anyone. You might recall that at the time of Jesus' birth,

Herod the Great had all the children in Bethlehem killed.[1] Herod Antipas, who followed his rule sometime later, agreed to behead John the Baptist after making a deceitful promise to his niece.[2]

Just preceding Paul's time at Antioch, Gaius Caesar ruled, also called Caligula. Biography.com has this to say about him:

"Tortured by headaches, Caligula wandered the palace at night. He abandoned the customary toga for silken gowns and often dressed as a woman. In addition, Caligula flaunted his power, eliminating his political rivals and forcing parents to watch the executions of their sons. Most egregious, however, was Caligula's declaration that he was a living God, ordering a bridge to be built between his palace and the Temple of Jupiter so that he could have consultations with the deity. Not even marriage and the birth of a daughter seemed to change him."[3]

Gaius was succeeded by Claudius, who expelled all the Jews from Rome. The Emperor Nero, who Paul appealed to in Acts 25:11, was equally harsh and ungodly. He put his own mother to death.[4]

These were unsaved, arrogant, destructive men with appalling behaviors. Paul spent time in prison for his faith under Roman rule, and the prisons of that day were exceedingly harsh, yet He echoed Jesus' words to SUBMIT to their authority.

---

[1] Mt 2:16
[2] Mk 6:25
[3] https://www.biography.com/political-figure/caligula
[4] https://www.thebiblejourney.org/biblejourney1/21-the-romanojewish-world-of-the-new-testament/roman-emperors-in-the-new-testament/; https://en.wikipedia.org/wiki/Nero

The Pharisees tried to trick Jesus into saying the wrong thing and so sent a group of men out to ask Him a question. "What do you think?" they asked. "Should we pay taxes to Caesar or not?"

They figured He would be unable to argue this point. If He said *no*, He'd be in trouble with the Romans. But Jesus was the wisdom of God.[5]

"But Jesus perceived their wickedness, and said, Why tempt ye me, ye hypocrites? Shew me the tribute money. And they brought unto him a penny. And he saith unto them, Whose is this image and superscription? They say unto him, Caesar's. Then saith he unto them, RENDER THEREFORE UNTO CAESAR THE THINGS WHICH ARE CAESAR'S*; and unto God the things that are God's."* (Matthew 22:18-21)

This was the second time He'd made such a comment. Five chapters earlier, we read where He was accused of not paying the temple tax, and He sent Peter out to get the needed coin from a fish's mouth. We need to see why.

"And when they were come to Capernaum, they that received tribute money came to Peter, and said, Doth not your master pay tribute? He saith, Yes. And when he was come into the house, Jesus prevented him, saying, What thinkest thou, Simon? of whom do the kings of the earth take custom or tribute? of their own children, or of strangers? Peter saith unto him, Of strangers. Jesus saith unto him, Then are the children free. Notwithstanding, LEST WE SHOULD OFFEND THEM, go thou to the sea, and cast an hook, and take up the fish that first cometh up; and when

---

[5] Lk 11:49; 1Co 1:30

thou hast opened his mouth, thou shalt find a piece of money: that take, and give unto them for me and thee." (Matthew 17:24-27)

Jesus refused to take a stance that anyone could misconstrue as REBELLION and OFFENSE. He didn't believe He owed the tax, but HE PAID IT ANYWAY.

I get it. In this time of blatant ungodliness, of politicians who lie, cheat, and steal, it's easy to get angry and push back. Because of what that man or woman stands for, because of what they believe in error, we disrespect the office. Or the flag. Or the national anthem. Those are included in our respect because they REPRESENT THE OFFICE.

It is one thing to stand against evil and another to break the law, to indulge in criticism, and to act in contempt and insolence, which is the motive behind such acts. We refuse to pray because we don't like the person placed over us. We not only TAKE OFFENSE, we propagate it. We plant seeds in the hearts of others, and the weeds spread to steal the Word from their heart.

We've failed to see that in Jesus' parable. The person planting the wrong seeds is often ourselves in someone else's soil. **The birds that steal the seed, the THIEVES AND ROBBERS, are me and you.**[6] It is US, members of the body of Christ, who discourage weaker people from right behaviors.[7]

SUBMISSON to authority applies to our mindsets about church pastors as well. It doesn't matter what you think about a minister of God from any denomination, whether you attend there or not. If he or she is the leader of a group of people, then God has placed him there, and he is

---

[6] Mt 13:4, 7
[7] Rm 14:21

considered a "higher power."

We are to SUBMIT. We are to PRAY, not criticize and make fun of. There is no place allowed in the Word of God for speaking against God's minister in any fashion.

"I exhort therefore, that, first of all, SUPPLICATIONS, PRAYERS, INTERCESSIONS, and GIVING OF THANKS, be made for all men; FOR KINGS, AND FOR ALL THAT ARE IN AUTHORITY; that we may lead a quiet and peaceable life in all godliness and honesty. For this is good and acceptable in the sight of God our Saviour." (1 Timothy 2:1-3)

We've heard this verse and maybe swallowed it like a lump of coal. Or maybe we've rejoiced in its words because it promises peace and quietness. But in that thought, PRAYER is how that PEACE comes, and that PRAYER, that INTERCESSION through the HOLY SPIRIT'S POWER, has no qualifications on it.

Not, "Pray because this is a godly man."

But, "Pray regardless." Even greater, **PRAY and GIVE THANKS.**

Here is what we overlook. If it's a man who is doing ungodly things, we cannot pray a curse. Remember? That isn't God's way. But God is well able to remove him from power and put him or her where they can do the least harm. He can also turn their hearts toward Him and bring repentance.

If it's a minister whose preaching untruths, then we turn him over to the God of TRUTH, who can and will correct him. God can reveal to him what he needs to know and give him understanding. But, however He does it in them or whatever He does with them, HE IS THE JUDGE, and in the end, our prayers will bring QUIET and PEACEFUL lives because of GODLINESS and HONESTY. Not because of hate and cruelty and rebellion.

Even the most despicable person was included in Jesus' victory over hell and the grave and His glorious Resurrection. He forgave a thief while in agony on the cross![8] Souls are won by LOVE. Governments are changed through PRAYER. Our behavior towards authority is an example of Christ to a dying world.

We are told to even guard our thoughts, that what we think about someone is what will come out our mouths and, greater, that it is as if we've already done the act we've pictured in our head.[9] Instead, our thoughts should be what is true, honest, just, pure, lovely, and of good report. They should hold virtue and give praise.[10] If they tear down instead of build up, then we are in the wrong.

The apostle Peter twice declared he'd defend Christ more than anyone else.[11] He came to regret those rash words. But what a change in his heart we can see when we read 1 Peter.

"SUBMIT YOURSELVES TO EVERY ORDINANCE OF MAN for the Lord's sake: whether it be to the king, as supreme; Or unto governors, as unto them that are sent by him for the punishment of evildoers, and for the praise of them that do well. For so is the will of God, that WITH WELL DOING ye may put to silence the ignorance of foolish men: As free, and NOT USING YOUR LIBERTY FOR A CLOKE OF MALICIOUSNESS, but as THE SERVANTS OF GOD. Honour all men. Love the brotherhood. Fear God. Honour the king." (1 Peter 2:13-17)

---

[8] Lk 23:42-43

[9] Pr 23:7; Mt 5:28

[10] Php 4:8

[11] Mt 16:22; Mt 26:35

These verses call SUBMISSION to authority, WELL DOING. They reiterate it by saying never to take freedom and use it for hate. **We are SERVANTS OF GOD, and as His representatives on earth, we must honor all men, especially those placed in authority over us.**

Let's also read this passage in the Passion Translation.

"In order to honor the Lord, you must RESPECT and DEFER to the authority of every human institution, whether it be the highest ruler or the governors he puts in place to punish lawbreakers and to praise those who do what's right. For it is God's will for you to silence the ignorance of foolish people by DOING WHAT IS RIGHT." (1 Peter 2:13-15 TPT)

We honor the Lord when we respect authority. It is God's will to do so. This is stated so clearly. But notice also, our motive must be right. We do it for the right reason and not out of insolence.

"Well, I paid my taxes, but ..." and then we go on, railing against it.

Instead, we are SUBMITTED, and we walk in love. We choose peace over strife. This is God's way. We cannot say we are children of God when peace is not ruling our thoughts, words, and actions.[12]

Peter goes on to describe the attitude of a servant toward his master, and his words make our behavior even clearer.

"Those who are servants, submit to the authority of those who are your masters—not only to those who are kind and gentle but EVEN TO THOSE WHO ARE HARD AND

---

[12] Col 3:15

DIFFICULT. You find God's favor by DECIDING TO PLEASE GOD even when you endure hardships because of unjust suffering." (1 Peter 2:18-19 TPT)

It doesn't matter if they are kind and gentle or if they are hard and difficult, our SUBMISSION is required! We decide to do it because that is God's instruction.

But know this, God isn't blind or deaf to any discomfort we are forced to live under. He saw the Israelites' bondage in Egypt, that they had to make bricks without straw. He heard their sorrows and had prepared, way in advance of it, a man to walk them out of Egypt in great deliverance.[13]

He saw Noah, a just man with a righteous family line. He heard his words of godliness to a wicked people and saved him and his family from complete destruction. He then honored Noah with the rainbow, as a covenant promise, and placed in the earth the law of seedtime and harvest.[14]

He knew that Joshua needed encouragement to enter Canaan and conquer its inhabitants. He gave Moses strong words of courage and strength to enable him to conquer his doubts.[15]

God sees you. God hears you. God answers prayer.[16]

Rebellion

When King Saul made the sacrifice in the prophet Samuel's stead, when he allowed impatience, fear, and pride to push him into sin and lost the kingship of Israel

---

[13] Ex 5:7, 18; Ex 2:5, 24; Ex 3:2

[14] Ge 6:8-9, 18; Ge 8:1, 22; Ge 9:1, 12-13

[15] Deu 1:38; Deu 3:28; Deu 31:7-8

[16] 1Pe 3:12

forever, Samuel made a statement that we cannot afford to overlook.

"And Samuel said, Hath the LORD as great delight in burnt offerings and sacrifices, as in OBEYING the voice of the LORD? Behold, TO OBEY is better than sacrifice, and TO HEARKEN than the fat of rams. FOR REBELLION IS AS THE SIN OF WITCHCRAFT, AND STUBBORNNESS IS AS INIQUITY AND IDOLATRY. Because thou hast rejected the word of the LORD, he hath also rejected thee from being king." (1 Samuel 15:22-23)

Every behavior has two sides, and the opposite of SUBMISSION is REBELLION. The prophet makes it plain, here, that REBELLION is a serious sin. He includes STUBBORNNESS alongside it.

The word "rebellion" means "bitterness" in both the Old and New Testaments.[17]

I find that incredibly apt. Someone rebels against authority because they've rehearsed an offense over and over in their mind until it has poisoned their words and actions. It has become a stronghold, a mental fortress,[18] and strongholds work against the knowledge of the ANOINTED ONE and the ANOINTING, remember?[19]

You cannot be in rebellion and bitterness and expect God to use you to DO GOOD and HEAL those OPPRESSED of the devil. With one word we quote Scripture, with another we call a lawmaker a name. This behavior simply cannot be![20]

The apostle Paul fully described the rebellious person

---

17 H4805; G4088

18 G3794

19 2Co 10:4-5

20 Jas 3:10-12

when speaking to the CHURCH at Rome.

"As it is written, There is none righteous, no, not one: There is none that understandeth, there is none that seeketh after God. They are all gone out of the way, they are together become UNPROFITABLE; there is NONE THAT DOETH GOOD, no, not one. Their throat is an open sepulchre; with their tongues they have used deceit; the poison of asps is under their lips: WHOSE MOUTH IS FULL OF CURSING AND BITTERNESS: Their feet are swift to shed blood: DESTRUCTION and MISERY are in their ways: And the way of peace have they not known: There is no fear of God before their eyes." (Romans 3:9-18)

A bitter man or woman doesn't seek after God. They are not righteous, and their unrighteous actions are unprofitable. Their words are poison. With them, they destroy people. They don't have peace or offer anyone peace but only misery. They have no reverence for God in the way they act.

They refuse to SUBMIT to God's commands. They will not DO GOOD. How serious that is.

In contrast, to the CHURCH at Ephesus, Paul compares a SUBMISSIVE Christian's behavior to a REBELLIOUS one's, and we can learn from it.

"Let no CORRUPT COMMUNICATION proceed out of your mouth, but that WHICH IS GOOD to the use of EDIFYING, that it may minister grace unto the hearers. And grieve not the holy Spirit of God, whereby ye are sealed unto the day of redemption. Let all bitterness, and wrath, and anger, and clamour, and evil speaking, be put away from you, with all malice: And BE YE KIND ONE TO ANOTHER, TENDERHEARTED, FORGIVING ONE ANOTHER, even as God

for Christ's sake hath forgiven you." (Ephesians 4:29-32)

Our rebellion grieves the Holy Spirit. Our corrupt words, our bitterness and anger, only work to increase hate. We must put these away from us. Far away. There is no God in them.

Instead, we are to edify, to be kind and forgiving. An instruction TO FORGIVE implies there will be occasions to be BITTER. We are instructed to let those go because bitterness and rebellion are products of evil.

Proverbs 17:11 states this plainly. *"An evil man seeketh only rebellion."*

Rebellion is a devilish state of the heart. We cannot justify it in ourselves nor make it equal with godliness. Yes, God had David fight against ungodly nations, ordering their destruction. God will set up men and women to stand up to corruption in governments. But that is just my point – God is behind it.

Rebellion, on the other hand, destroys what God has created, whether that is an organization, a nation, or a church. It is a form of witchcraft. Witchcraft is worshipping another being, whether human or supernatural, as god. It takes the glory away from the Creator, from the Savior of mankind, and places it on something else.

It is listed in Galatians 5:19-21 with other "works of the flesh." These are sinful, ungodly behaviors.

"Now the works of the flesh are manifest, which are these; Adultery, fornication, uncleanness, lasciviousness, Idolatry, witchcraft, hatred, variance, emulations, wrath, strife, seditions, heresies, Envyings, murders, drunkenness, revellings, and such like: of the which I tell you before, as I have also told you in time past, that THEY WHICH DO SUCH THINGS SHALL NOT INHERIT THE KINGDOM OF GOD."

That's quite a list! We won't define them all, but we must notice how they are all listed as being against God.

Vincent's Word Studies says, "The kingdom of God is, essentially, the absolute dominion of God in the universe, both in a physical and a spiritual sense. It is 'an organic commonwealth which has the principle of its existence in the will of God.' (Tholuck)."[21]

That clarifies things well. God's will is what is done in His kingdom. **Rebellion like witchcraft, is choosing your will instead. It is doing what YOU WANT to do, not what GOD IS ASKING.**

1 Corinthians 6:10 gives another list of behaviors that go against God's will. Notice, these are all considered UNRIGHTEOUSNESS. Then it says, *"Be not deceived,"* implying you can be. You can believe any of these unrighteous behaviors are okay and are not sinful.

"Know ye not that the UNRIGHTEOUS shall not inherit the kingdom of God? Be not deceived: neither fornicators, nor idolaters, nor adulterers, nor effeminate, nor abusers of themselves with mankind, Nor thieves, nor covetous, nor drunkards, nor revilers, nor extortioners, shall inherit the kingdom of God." (1 Corinthians 6:9-10)

Turn on the news or secular TV and you will see people DECEIVED about these behaviors all the time, but such deception is not part of the KINGDOM OF GOD.

God's children, His people, are not to behave this way.

"And such were some of you: but ye are washed, but ye are sanctified, but ye are justified in the name of the Lord

---

[21] Lk 6:20

Jesus, and by the Spirit of our God." (1 Corinthians 6:11)

You have been washed in the blood of Christ. You have been sanctified, or set apart as holy, for God's use through JESUS' NAME. You have been FORGIVEN and placed in God's kingdom by the HOLY SPIRIT'S power. Now, "Acts" like it!

Because rebellion ALWAYS affects other people. That is the heart of it. How we act affects the strength or weakness of those around us. Rebellion grows corrupt fruit.

In Florida, a bacterium called "greening" will destroy an entire grove in no time. The fruit never ripens and eventually falls to the ground. Over time, the trees will die.

This is a vivid picture of rebellion. The hatred in one man's heart soon spreads to many more and OFFENSE takes hold, fueled by selfishness and the devil's deception.

"FOLLOW PEACE with all men, and HOLINESS, without which no man shall see the Lord: Looking diligently lest any man fail of the grace of God; LEST ANY ROOT OF BITTERNESS SPRINGING UP TROUBLE YOU, and THEREBY MANY BE DEFILED." (Hebrews 12:14-15)

Suddenly, what we've harbored to ourselves becomes something spread through others, and having taken hold, rebellion will destroy everyone around it.

It becomes a battle cry. "Look at what was done to me!"

Clinging to unforgiveness in our hearts, we destroy everyone around us.

This is not the purpose of the church. We are to FOLLOW PEACE. We are to GO out in JESUS' NAME and stretch a hand to HEAL. We are to see people set FREE, to PREACH DELIVERANCE, and to CAST OUT demonic

OPPRESSION.

Not to take part in it.

Daniel

An excellent example of the proper attitude toward government is found in the life of Daniel. We can learn much about dependence on God in difficult circumstances by studying him.

In Daniel, chapter 1, the kingdom of Babylon has conquered Israel and taken a number of their young men captive. Daniel and his friends, Hananiah, Mishael, and Azariah, have been placed in training to become members of King Nebuchadnezzar's court.

We'll read it from the Voice Translation.

"After the king returned home, he commanded Ashpenaz, chief of the royal eunuchs, to bring some of the Israelites who had been taken captive to the palace. These included members of Judah's royal family and the nobility. He was looking for potential candidates from the exiles to serve in his court, fit young men with no physical or moral infirmities, handsome, skilled in all wisdom, knowledgeable, discerning, and understanding. Those selected would be taught the language and literature of the Chaldeans, the people who lived in Babylonia. As part of THEIR ASSIMILATION INTO BABYLONIAN COURT LIFE, the king offered them a daily portion of food and wine from his own table. They were to be educated for three years before serving in the king's court. From among Judah's exiles, Daniel, Hananiah, Mishael, and Azariah were selected. Ashpenaz, chief of the royal eunuchs, gave them Babylonian names to signify their new identities in a foreign place: Daniel he renamed Belteshazzar; Hananiah, Shadrach;

Mishael, Meshach; and Azariah, Abed-nego." (Daniel 1:3-8)

The Voice Translation's commentary points out that the taking of captives was a way to subjugate the nation that had been conquered and forcing them to learn the Babylonian language, as well as to dine on its foods and worship its gods, was a way of destroying the conquered nation's culture. This is what Daniel and his friends faced. Their entire way of life was being destroyed and the God they believed in disregarded.

They knew this when offered the king's food. It was also likely the meat had been sacrificed to false gods. So their reason for abstaining was one of spiritual integrity.

Let me remind you of Paul's words, which we referred to in an earlier chapter.

"Let's say a person (someone who knows of Jesus) sees you eating in the temple of an idol; and because the person with a weaker conscience is still unsure of things, he becomes confident, follows your lead, and eats idol food. Now, because of your knowledge on display in your conduct, the weaker brother or sister—for whom the Anointed One died—is destroyed! Ruined! What's more, by living according to your knowledge, you have sinned against these brothers and sisters and wounded their weak consciences—and because you sinned against them, you have sinned against the Anointed One, the Liberating King. So if any type of food is an issue that causes my brothers and sisters to fall away from God, then God forbid I should ever eat it again so that I would never be the crack, the rise, or the rock on the road that causes them to stumble." (1 Corinthians 8:10-13)

Daniel and his friends refused to partake of the king's meat, but their refusal wasn't rebellion. Rebellion, as we've said, is a bitter attitude of the heart. They weren't refusing in order to cause strife or to shame anyone. They were being obedient to God's law and that obedience required taking a stand against the king's wishes.

"Although the king ate only the finest Babylonian fare, Daniel was determined NOT TO VIOLATE GOD'S LAW AND DEFILE HIMSELF by eating the food and drinking the wine that came from the king's table; so he asked the chief of the royal eunuchs for permission not to eat the food. Now GOD HAD GIVEN DANIEL SPECIAL FAVOR and fondness in the eyes of the king's chief eunuch. Still the eunuch was concerned." (Daniel 1:8-9)

Notice, God had given Daniel favor. This is another sign that they weren't in rebellion but in obedience. Where obedience is required, God will always be with you. He will instruct you in what to say, what actions to take, and give you any wisdom and understanding you need.

God can make a way where there isn't one. He is the God of the impossible.[22] Also, the Holy Spirit in us and upon us, through the baptism in the Holy Spirit, will give us what to say when we need to say it. This is a promise of Christ based on our obedience.[23]

Daniel asked, in obedience to the command of God, to be given only vegetables and grains. The eunuch spoke his doubts about the wisdom of this, so Daniel suggested a 10-day trial period. If they looked healthy at the end of it, then they should be allowed to continue with their altered diet. This seemed agreeable to the eunuch, and of course, as the story goes, God blessed the four Jewish youths with so

---

[22] Is 43:19; Lk 1:37
[23] Mk 13:11, 13

much health that when the trial period was over, everyone else was put on their diet too![24]

Plus, they were blessed with great wisdom and understanding, which got them noticed.[25]

"When the king inquired further into their grasp of wisdom and understanding, he discovered that they were better prepared than all the magicians and enchanters in his empire, even 10 times better. This is how Daniel came to serve the royal court, a position he safely held until the first year of King Cyrus when his Persian army conquered Babylonia." (Daniel 1:20-21 VOICE)

Such is God's way. Our submission to God will always turn out better than anything we try to do in our own efforts. Daniel chose to let God take care of them when he could have acted out in any number of ways. He could have made a scene and called the king names. He could have complained to all the others around him. He could have refused to eat the king's meat AS AN ACT OF REBELLION instead of being submitted and obedient. Think about that. What if he'd demanded to not eat meat and made fun of the king?

He didn't do that. He didn't say, "You've got some nerve, after all you've done to my people." What a much different end there would have been to the story!

Daniel and his friends were continually blessed by God. I encourage you to read the book of Daniel, chapters 1 through 6, on your own. The thread which ties their lives together, from salvation in the fiery furnace to Daniel's survival of the lion's den, is that they submitted to the king's

---

[24] Dan 1:15-16

[25] Dan 1:17

office yet stayed obedient to God's law.

God delivered them each time and honored them with high positions in the kingdom well into the reign of the kings that followed. They had far more influence by staying at peace than they would ever have had by choosing strife. In fact, King Nebuchadnezzar threatened to kill all his magicians, including Daniel, if one of them couldn't tell him *what* he had dreamed, as well as what that dream meant. It was when the others failed that Daniel stepped in and saved them all – the godly AND the ungodly.

"The Chaldeans were correct. There are no wise men, enchanters, magicians, or sorcerers in all the world who are able to reveal the mystery the king requested. BUT THERE IS A GOD IN HEAVEN WHO CAN REVEAL SUCH MYSTERIES. The dream you dreamed and the visions you saw, King Nebuchadnezzar, unveil the future and disclose what will happen at the end of the age. Now I will tell you what you dreamed and the visions you saw as you slept in your bed."

Good king, as you lay in your bed that night, thoughts about the future sprang up in your mind, and the revealer of all mysteries unveiled to you what is going to happen. I AM HERE TODAY, NOT BECAUSE I HAVE GREATER WISDOM THAN ANY OTHER IN THE LAND, BUT BECAUSE GOD IN HIS WISDOM HAS REVEALED THIS MYSTERY TO ME. It is God's plan that the king knows the meaning of this dream and understands the thoughts that raced through your mind." (Daniel 2:27-30 VOICE)

What a phenomenal testimony that is! But know this, he didn't pitch a fit over how the kingdom ran first. He didn't call them out on what idols they worshipped. He didn't condemn how the Babylonians ate or make fun of their lifestyle. He lived with them as he'd been told to do, humbly, and in fact, the prophet Jeremiah had spoken a word from God to all the captured people of Israel, stating they must live there in peace.

We are familiar with Jeremiah 29:11, *"For I know the thoughts that I think toward you, saith the LORD, thoughts of peace, and not of evil, to give you an expected end."* This is an amazing promise to people living in unexpected captivity. But let's reverse and read what comes before it.

Verse 1 says, *"Now these are the words of the letter that Jeremiah the prophet sent from Jerusalem unto the residue of the elders which were CARRIED AWAY CAPTIVES, and to the priests, and to the prophets, and TO ALL THE PEOPLE whom Nebuchadnezzar had carried away captive from Jerusalem to Babylon."* This confirms these words were for Daniel and his friends.

Now, let's read verses 4-7.

"Thus saith the LORD of hosts, the God of Israel, unto all that are carried away captives, whom I have caused to be carried away from Jerusalem unto Babylon; Build ye houses, and dwell in them; and plant gardens, and eat the fruit of them; Take ye wives, and beget sons and daughters; and take wives for your sons, and give your daughters to husbands, that they may bear sons and daughters; that ye may be increased there, and not diminished. And SEEK THE PEACE OF THE CITY whither I have caused you to be carried away captives, AND PRAY UNTO THE LORD FOR IT: for in the peace thereof shall ye have peace." (Jeremiah 29:4-7)

How incredible that is! The captives were to SEEK PEACE and, even greater, to PRAY for Babylon. They were not to rebel and criticize and argue.

If you read the remainder of the chapter, there is a warning against prophets who had spoken otherwise. Some had prophesied falsely that instead of 70 years in captivity it would be only a few. They encouraged rebellion, and God was displeased with this.[26]

The captives were, instead, to increase and prosper there. IN BABYLON. In CAPTIVITY.

Daniel and his friends chose peace. They chose to obey the rules of a foreign country that had destroyed their cities and plundered their temple. Think about that. What great grace that took! They submitted to their lives to the king of Babylon, EXCEPT when what the king decreed asked them to disobey God. In that moment, they took a stand for their faith, but they did it correctly, with wisdom.

Joseph

Much is told about Joseph, his coat of many colors, and his prophetic dreams, but they are only a portion of a much larger picture. A key element of his life illustrates our behavior as members of the church. In order to understand it, we must start at the beginning.

Joseph was his father's favorite son, the youngest of 12. As if that wasn't enough to create friction with his brothers, age 17, he made a serious error in judgment. God gave him a series of dreams about his future, but instead of holding them close to his heart, he told his brothers every detail.

Hate entered their hearts, and they decided to kill him but make it look like a wild animal was responsible. The oldest brother, Reuben, didn't want to take things that far and so offered an alternative plan. They'd put Joseph in a pit and leave him there. In his mind, he figured he could sneak back when the others weren't looking and set Joseph free.[27]

---

[26] Jer 29:8-10
[27] Ge 37:21-22

His brother must've realized this at some point because after lying to their dad about Joseph's death, they spotted some slave traders and decided to sell him instead.[28]

Now, let me point out that Joseph ended up in this mess through his own bad judgment. The Scriptures do not say why God gave him those dreams at such a young age. Know too that God wasn't unfamiliar with Joseph's personality. We don't know how God expected Joseph to react at such an incredible prophecy, but the story of Joseph's bondage in Egypt is where I want to pick up.

He was sold to Potiphar, captain of the guard, and the Bible says:

"The Eternal One was with Joseph, however, and HE BECAME SUCCESSFUL in his own right AS A SLAVE within the house of his Egyptian master. Potiphar could not help but notice that the Eternal One was with Joseph and CAUSED EVERYTHING JOSEPH DID TO PROSPER. Joseph became the favorite of the household and rose in the ranks to become Potiphar's personal attendant. In time, Potiphar made Joseph overseer of the entire household and put him in charge of everything he owned. From that moment, the Eternal One blessed the Egyptian's house for Joseph's sake, a blessing which seemed to cover everything Potiphar possessed from house to field." (Genesis 39:2-5 VOICE)

Did you hear that? Joseph was successful AS A SLAVE. He PROSPERED as a SLAVE.

Egypt was not Joseph's country, and the Egyptians were not his people. He was stuck there because his brothers betrayed him! Yet instead of showing rebellion and

---

[28] Ge 37:25-29

resentment, Joseph served well beneath the government he'd been given. He served SO WELL that he caused Potiphar's goods to be abundantly blessed!

I have to pause and ask if we could do the same. Could we serve those who were seemingly our enemies but still maintain our faith? Would we get there and, instead, spend all our time going over and over our lot in life?

Life is not always a smooth, level path. I wish it was. I've always said I wanted my life to be a straight line, no failures but also no successes. I'd rather it was one boring, safe existence. That is completely unrealistic, I know, because having FAITH requires EXERCISING IT. Faith is not faith without taking action, and most of the time, that action means we are in need. (Jas 2:20) Something isn't as it should be for us, yet we honor God's instructions and refuse to complain. We turn our problem over to God and keep our attitudes right.

Joseph's attitude was right. He walked in obedience to God and was submissive to his master.

We can see this fully as the story unfolds. Potiphar's wife had eyes for Joseph and tried to seduce him on more than one occasion. Each time, he refused.

"Look, please don't take offense, but with me in charge, my master has no concerns for anything that goes on in his house. He has trusted me with everything he has. He hasn't treated me like I am any less than he is, and he hasn't kept anything from me—except, of course, for you because you are his wife. Why would I do something so clearly wrong and sin so blatantly against God?" (Genesis 39:8-9)

Here's a difficult situation. God has blessed him abundantly in Potiphar's household, and he will not go against the law of God, but at the same time, Potiphar's wife refuses to back off. He can hardly accuse her to anyone. He's a slave. How will that look? He opts for avoidance at first, refusing to be left alone with her.[29]

This was wisdom, but it would not protect him in the long run. One day, he comes inside to do business, and she corners him. Panicked, Joseph pulls free of her and flees. In the struggle, he leaves his coat behind, and the wickedness in her heart sets the trap.[30]

We cannot always avoid potholes. There will be opportunities to sin and other times when we find ourselves in a dark place through no fault of our own. Psalm 23 says, *"Yea, though I walk THROUGH the valley of the shadow of death, I will fear no evil."*[31] "Through" means in one side and out the other. That's wonderful news, but it also means at one point, we were standing directly in the center.

Joseph found himself accused of something he did not do and standing in prison for it. He's gone from favored son to hated brother to Egyptian slave to prosperous servant, and now he's at the bottom again. What an incredible opportunity to hate his life. He could have chosen, justifiably, to curse his situation and everyone who put him there.

Except he didn't, and that choice would, in time, save an entire nation.

"But the Eternal One remained with Joseph and showed him His loyal love and granted him FAVORED STATUS with the chief jailor. The jailor put Joseph in charge of all of the prisoners who were confined there. WHATEVER NEEDED TO BE DONE, JOSEPH WAS THE ONE TO DO IT. The

---

[29] Ge 39:10

[30] Ge 39:11-12

[31] Ps 23:4

chief jailor, like Potiphar, didn't need to worry about anything that was in Joseph's care because the Eternal One was with him. And WHATEVER JOSEPH DID WORKED OUT WELL because the Eternal made it so." (Genesis 39:21-23)

How amazing that is. Even at his lowest moment, Joseph did whatever needed to be done. He kept his attitude right, and God prospered him. IN PRISON.

Paul and Silas found themselves in prison unjustly and instead of complaining about how they got there, instead of talking badly about the magistrates who'd tossed them inside, they chose to praise God.[32]

"And suddenly there was a great earthquake, so that the foundations of the prison were shaken: and immediately all the doors were opened, and every one's bands were loosed." (Acts 16:26)

God literally set them free because of their submission.

More importantly, when the jail cell door opened, they didn't try to escape. They were physically FREE but CHOSE TO SUBMIT to authority. They let God give them justice.[33]

Plus, the jailer and his entire household were saved because of how they acted![34]

Joseph's submission to authority was part of his submission to God. Paul's and Silas' submission to the jailer was their submission to God. Now consider Daniel's words to King Nebuchadnezzar again.

---

[32] Acts 16:20-21, 25

[33] Act 16:35-36

[34] Act 16:34

"Good king, as you lay in your bed that night, THOUGHTS ABOUT THE FUTURE sprang up in your mind, and the REVEALER OF ALL MYSTERIES UNVEILED TO YOU WHAT IS GOING TO HAPPEN. I am here today, not because I have greater wisdom than any other in the land, but because God in His wisdom has revealed this mystery to me." (Daniel 2:29-30 VOICE)

God knows the future. He set Joseph up to be the ruler of Pharaoh's storehouses, a position which would bring reconciliation with his family and great deliverance. He placed Daniel within the king's court to interpret his dream and eventually turn his heart toward the true God.[35]

We only see the steps directly in front of us and in our humanness could make terrible mistakes. **But God sees the entire picture and asks of us faith, patience, and obedience.**

Let's read Jeremiah 29:6-7 once more, this time in the Voice Translation.

"During these years of captivity, let your families grow and not die out. PURSUE THE PEACE AND WELFARE OF THE CITY where I sent you into exile. PRAY TO ME, THE ETERNAL, FOR BABYLON because if it has peace, you will live in peace.'"

Pray for Babylon. We will not find another more powerful, humbling instruction than that. Our feelings about being in exile do not matter. Our feelings about the government where we live do not matter. Our likes and dislikes of their style of leadership do not matter. What we are falsely accused of does not matter. If we've been

[35] Dan 4:37

demoted through the devil's work, it does not matter. Nothing matters but maintaining a godly attitude, walking in obedience to God's will at that moment, and dedicating ourselves to prayer.

Those prayers will change things.

Chapter 12

The Generous Church

We sing the familiar altar call song, eyes closed, the words locked in our memory.

"I surrender all. I surrender all." Yet we only partially mean its words. "I surrender all, except when it comes to my attitude."

"All to thee, my blessed Savior. I surrender all."[1] Except for my finances. We make an excuse to control the "important" things.

We pray for revival but refuse to become vessels of honor, fit for the Master's use.[2] What we really want is a spectacular display of weirdness to talk about. We want Brother Jones to run around the aisles, flailing his arms, and Sister Sam to stand up and caw like a crow. Then we can get a chuckle and go home and lie in bed as selfish as we were before.

God desires WILLING and OBEDIENT hearts.[3] Willing to check your attitude at the door, willing to submit to God's command to LOVE ONE ANOTHER,[4] and the right ATTITUDE about giving. We are SUBMISSIVE in every area, not those we pick and choose.

Revival means something that was dead, something we allowed to die which we should have kept alive, has been made ALIVE again. It means we have had a CHANGE of heart. **We will no longer be how we've been that caused the things of God to fade inside us, but we will walk after**

---

[1] "I Surrender All" by Judson W. Van de Venter (1855-1939)

[2] 2Ti 2:20-21

[3] Is 1:19

[4] Jn 13:34; Jn 15:12; 1Jn 4:7

God PASSIONATELY from now on.

It's a PERMANENT change not a temporary one.

Revival means REPENTANCE, and repentance requires sincerity, openness, and humility. You cannot pretend to repent. God will see right through that.

Since God alone knows the heart, since God sees what's done in secret, since He makes darkness shine as noonday, we waste our time trying to pull the wool over His eyes. He wants no more vain, meaningless, insincere worshippers.[5]

"To what purpose is the multitude of your sacrifices unto me? saith the LORD: I am full of the burnt offerings of rams, and the fat of fed beasts; and I delight not in the blood of bullocks, or of lambs, or of he goats. When ye come to appear before me, who hath required this at your hand, to tread my courts? BRING NO MORE VAIN OBLATIONS; incense is an abomination unto me; the new moons and sabbaths, the calling of assemblies, I cannot away with; it is iniquity, even the solemn meeting. Your new moons and your appointed feasts my soul hateth: they are a trouble unto me; I am weary to bear them. And when ye spread forth your hands, I will hide mine eyes from you: yea, when ye make many prayers, I will not hear: your hands are full of blood. WASH YOU, MAKE YOU CLEAN; put away the evil of your doings from before mine eyes; cease to do evil; Learn to do well; seek judgment, relieve the oppressed, judge the fatherless, plead for the widow. Come now, and let us reason together, saith the LORD: though your sins be as scarlet, they shall be as white as snow; though they be red like crimson, they shall be as wool. If ye be WILLING AND OBEDIENT, ye shall eat the good of the land." (Isaiah 1:11-19)

---

[5] Ps 44:21; 1Jn 3:20; Mt 6:4, 18; Ps 37:6

If we want to see a move of God, if we want to experience the presence of God and do the things of God, then we must become the people of God. In every area. We must submit where we'd rather not, as well as where it's easy, and continually search our hearts for any remnants of rebellion. We must stay connected to the Vine in order to find joy and success. To accept God's words about grace and reject His command to honor government is like cutting yourself free of the roots.

Offense kills the power of God. Unforgiveness prevents DUNAMIS from working. Stubbornness makes all our worship in vain. These must be revealed to us, and we must determine to REPENT of them. Yet still there is another area that will keep us from being THE CHURCH of Acts. To be who God wants us to be, to GO and DO as He has commanded, we have to relinquish our hold on money.

Our attitude about giving and finances can stop us in our tracks.

The Tithe

Mention money in the church and the claws come out. The fact anyone reacts negatively to Bible truths about finances tells me how much REBELLION there is in the church over the issue. People do not want to SUBMIT their wallets to God.

Statistics bear this out. Only 3%-5% of church-going Americans tithe regularly, yet 17% of those surveyed say they do.[6] What an incredible fact. 12% lie about tithing. The other 97% don't give at all.

GIVING is part of SUBMISSION, and NOT GIVING will prevent DUNAMIS from working in your life as much as taking OFFENSE.

---

[6] https://nonprofitssource.com/online-giving-statistics/church-giving/)

The tithe goes way back in biblical history. It is a definite command of Scripture. The price for rebellion against the tithe is equally noted.

The word "tithe" means "a tenth part." (H4643) The first reference to giving a tithe is from the life of Abraham, who gave a tenth of his goods (which were substantial) to the king of Salem, Melchizedek.[7] It is also mentioned by Jacob after his dream of a ladder ascending to heaven. He said, *"And of all that thou shalt give me I will surely give the tenth unto thee."*[8]

Instructions on tithing appear in Leviticus 27:30-32 and in Numbers 28:26 where it is called "firstfruits." This is important. It is not just that we give but that we give our first and best fruits. Bearing fruit is an analogy about success repeated in the Scriptures,[9] going as far back as the creation of man where the Triune God commanded man and woman to "be fruitful."[10]

Nehemiah 10:34-37 ties both words, "tithe" and "firstfruits," together.

But the concept of giving the best sacrifice to God goes back even further to Cain and Abel. Abel gave the best of the flock. Cain gave his offering as an afterthought, and God rejected it. In fact, God referred to what he'd given as sin.[11] We need look no further to Cain's attitude about the sacrifice than his reaction, killing his brother.[12]

Our attitude about giving is paramount. The most commonly read verses in regard to the tithe are actually about ATTITUDE and not money.

---

[7] Ge 14:20
[8] Ge 28:22
[9] Jn 15:4, 8
[10] Ge 1:22, 28
[11] Ge 4:4-7
[12] Ge 4:8

In Luke 6:38, we read:

"Give, and it shall be given unto you; good measure, pressed down, and shaken together, and running over, shall men give into your bosom. For with the same measure that ye mete withal it shall be measured to you again."

We must take this verse in context. What is being given? The preceding verses talk about loving our neighbor.[13] We are to love our enemies to the point we give them the shirt off our back. We are to be merciful in the same measure that God is merciful. We are NOT to judge one another, then the love we sow into other people's lives will return to us in abundance.

This works both positively and negatively. If we give judgment and anger and strife, that is what we will receive. That's not to say what we give financially is not included in the thought here, but the attitude behind the giving is what is of importance.

Another verse commonly used in regard to giving is Malachi 3:10.

"Bring ye all the tithes into the storehouse, that there may be meat in mine house, and prove me now herewith, saith the LORD of hosts, if I will not open you the windows of heaven, and pour you out a blessing, that there shall not be room enough to receive it."

Verses 11-12 go on to say those that tithe will be successful and protected from failure. God speaks blessing over obedience in giving. But here again, we have missed the context. All of Malachi is a stern warning to Israel for

---

[13] Lk 6:27-37

their neglect of and sins in regard to the sacrifice. Repeatedly, God says he will reject what they give because their sacrificial animal is lame and sick, because they complain about doing it, and because of their continuous sins.[14]

Malachi 3:10 is a plea of God's mercy for His people to stop making excuses and repent. It follows verses 8-9, which say:

"Will a man rob God? Yet ye have robbed me. But ye say, Wherein have we robbed thee? IN TITHES AND OFFERINGS. Ye are cursed with a curse: for ye have robbed me, even this whole nation." (Malachi 3:8-9)

And it comes before verses 13-15.

"Your words have been stout against me, saith the LORD. Yet ye say, What have we spoken so much against thee? Ye have said, IT IS VAIN TO SERVE GOD: and WHAT PROFIT IS IT THAT WE HAVE KEPT HIS ORDINANCE, and that we have walked mournfully before the LORD of hosts? And now we call the proud happy; yea, they that work wickedness are set up; yea, they that tempt God are even delivered." (Malachi 3:13-15)

Giving simply to be seen for giving, giving to GET something from God, giving because we feel guilty for not giving, and giving with sin in our hearts are all WRONG ATTITUDES.

Jesus noted this one day while observing those in the temple. Rich men entered, making a show of their gifts, and then a poor widow gave a small amount, money-wise, but

---

[14] Mal 1:7-8, 13; Mal 2:13, 17

with a different attitude. Jesus said, *"Of a truth I say unto you, that this poor widow HATH CAST IN MORE than they all: For all these have of their abundance cast in unto the offerings of God: but she of her penury hath cast in all the living that she had."*[15]

This doesn't mean that God requires everything we make but it is the ATTITUDE of WILLINGNESS He is looking for. I get it. You work hard, and it seems like every dollar is gone before you blink. You think about how you could use this money for other things, so it becomes painful to give. If you convince yourself to give, then the devil plays riot with your thoughts, convincing you it was a waste.

How can we become the giver described by the apostle Paul?

"Every man according AS HE PURPOSETH in his heart, so let him give; NOT GRUDGINGLY, or of necessity: for God loveth A CHEERFUL GIVER." (2 Corinthians 9:2)

It's all God's money anyhow.

Two truths from the Scriptures set me free in the area of finances and tithing. One was a revelation about stewardship.

What's a steward? The word "steward" in the Greek means "a house distributor (that is, manager), or overseer, that is, an employee in that capacity; by extension a fiscal agent (treasurer)."[16] It is someone who runs things for the boss. He pays the employees and sees to all other financial transactions, as well as doing many forms of office management.

---

[15] Lk 21:3-4
[16] G3623

Jesus referred to a wise and faithful steward[17] and also to an unjust steward who had wasted his master's things.[18] So we know, you can be a good steward or a terrible one.

But in either case, the steward ISN'T THE BOSS, merely the manager. He does a job for the OWNER. It's NOT his money being spent. In fact, doing more than what the owner has asked, spending money that he has no authority to spend is fraud and theft. Watch any reality crime show program and you will see cases where people tucked away money that belonged to their employer and were subsequently arrested.

Everything we earn belongs to God. This reality freed me from worries about money. If it belongs to God, then God will provide what I need when I need it. It's His responsibility. Not mine.

Think of it this way, what we own we treasure and protect. If we built a new house, we want it kept in its best shape. Its care becomes our job. Someone who is renting a home, however, doesn't have that attitude. It's not theirs. If there is a repair needed, they call the landlord – the OWNER.

Taking another view, if the OWNER of a business is hit with a huge bill, the house manager doesn't feel the same way about what's owed as the owner does. A steward will still be paid his salary, but the owner looks at it as an expense. It's his money that must be spent to cover the debt.

A preacher gave this example of stewardship. He gave $100 to a friend then instructed his friend to pass the money on to someone else. "Why do you think my friend

---

[17] Lk 12:42

[18] Lk 16:1, 8

isn't upset about giving the money away?" he asked. "Because it isn't his money to start with. Also, if he needs more, he knows who the source is."

How clear that is!

God is our source. We've looked at our bank accounts as if *we* were the source. It's what we've gained or lost through *our own* efforts. But the truth is, the job we have, the money we earn, the car we drive, all of it is God's. If we place it in God's control and are faithful to give as He's instructed, then money becomes nothing to worry about.

We are not CARELESS, but CAREFREE.

We have a relationship with God. Jesus lives in us, and the Holy Spirit leads us in all areas of our lives. He directs us where to work, how to act while we work there, and we obey the Word of God and are faithful to tithe of the FIRSTFRUITS. Only by being faithful in a small matter like money will our Master, the Source, trust us with more important things.

"If you're faithful in small-scale matters, you'll be faithful with far bigger responsibilities. If you're crooked in small responsibilities, you'll be no different in bigger things. If you can't even handle a small thing like money, who's going to entrust you with spiritual riches that really matter? If you don't manage well someone else's assets that are entrusted to you, who's going to give over to you important spiritual and personal relationships to manage?" (Luke 16:10-12 VOICE)

How powerful that is. Jesus goes on to say we can't serve God and money: *"Imagine you're a servant and you have two masters giving you orders. What are you going to do when they have conflicting demands? You can't serve both, so you'll either hate the first and love the second, or you'll faithfully serve the first and despise the second. ONE MASTER IS GOD AND THE OTHER IS MONEY. YOU CAN'T SERVE THEM BOTH."*[19]

We must choose who to serve. We will either follow after our fleshly lust for money and things, or we will follow God in submission.[20]

We can trust the Holy Spirit to give us wisdom for the use of our finances.[21] He will provide what we need for any situation we face. After all, this is the same God who rescued His people with all the riches of Egypt in their grasp, and what an amazing example that is![22]

Yet still, there is another element we must learn.

The Generous Heart

Deuteronomy 15 is a chapter of instructions about the Old Testament *year of release*. This occurred every seven years and commanded that all debts people owed you must be forgiven.[23]

The entire passage gives details of how to forgive the debt, speaking clearly on the attitude behind their obedience. How powerful that is. It wasn't simply they must forgive WHAT was owed but they must forgive it GENEROUSLY.

"But if there are any poor Israelites in your towns when you arrive in the land the Lord your God is giving you, DO NOT BE HARD-HEARTED OR TIGHTFISTED toward them. Instead, BE GENEROUS and lend them whatever they need. DO NOT BE MEAN-SPIRITED and refuse someone a loan

---

[19] Lk 16:13 VOICE
[20] Mk 4:19
[21] Eph 1:17
[22] Ex 12:35-36
[23] Deut 15:1

because the year for canceling debts is close at hand. If you refuse to make the loan and the needy person cries out to the Lord, you will be considered guilty of sin. GIVE GENEROUSLY to the poor, NOT GRUDGINGLY, for the Lord your God will bless you in everything you do." (Deuteronomy 15:7-10)

To hold a grudge means having ill-will and resentment. When we are "grudging," we are reluctant, even unwilling, to do something for someone else, regardless of the rightness of it or the poverty of their circumstances.[24]

Does that sound like our Savior's attitude toward us? One thousand times no!

In fact, Ephesians 4:19-20 says greediness is not like Christ at all. The verses following go on to tell us to renew our minds to think differently, to speak differently, to BE different people. It ends with, *"And be ye kind one to another, tenderhearted, forgiving one another, even as God for Christ's sake hath forgiven you."*[25]

Forgiveness is the number one evidence of God's grace at work in us. We have been forgiven much and so should forgive much. In this same thread, we have been blessed with much, so we should bless others to that measure.

I can say truthfully, my parents and my older brother have set the finest example. I cannot list in one book the number of generous things they have done for me and for others nor how faithful they have been to tithe, as God has directed.

My life is blessed because of how they have blessed

---

[24] Dictionary.com

[25] Eph 4:32

me, and I seek to be a blessing of that magnitude. I give away my books all the time, without any thought. I've bought groceries for friends and strangers when they were in need. I say this not as bragging but as an example of simple things you can do. And how FREEING it is to not expect anything in return!

It is amazing to give and not *regret* the giving. How incredible to have joy in it. This is our heavenly Father's will for us. **We should echo His generous, abundant heart or we are not the PASSIONATE CHURCH.**

We see this further in Deuteronomy 15:12-15.

"If a fellow Hebrew sells himself or herself to be your servant and serves you for six years, in the seventh year you must set that servant free. When you release a male servant, DO NOT SEND HIM AWAY EMPTY-HANDED. Give him A GENEROUS FAREWELL GIFT from your flock, your threshing floor, and your winepress. SHARE WITH HIM SOME OF THE BOUNTY with which the Lord your God has blessed you. REMEMBER that you were once slaves in the land of Egypt and the Lord your God redeemed you! That is why I am giving you this command." (NLT)

"Don't forget who you were, it says, and be generous to that amount! You were redeemed from slavery; now, you redeem others."

Such a wonderful word from God. But we must also read verse 18 to gain a full revelation. This thought really set me free. We are not to be grudging and tightfisted. We are to be generous. But also, we should not GRIEVE the loss of our gift.

"YOU MUST NOT CONSIDER IT A HARDSHIP when you release your servants. Remember that for six years they have

given you services worth double the wages of hired workers, and the Lord your God will bless you in all you do." (Deuteronomy 15:18 NLT)

Oh, how I identify with that mindset! How many times did I want to be generous, but I couldn't swallow the dollar amount? I have promised to do things for others then thought, "Why ... why did you say that, Suzanne?" I had so much GRIEF, as if I'd traded in my right arm. I *wanted* to enjoy the giving but didn't.

Here's the freedom, the nugget of truth that made the difference in me—**When we realize we are simply a STEWARD and NOT the OWNER, when we don't consider it OURS to GIVE AWAY, then there is no grief.** Just like that pastor's illustration, his friend had no problem passing the money along because it wasn't his. He didn't VALUE it as AN OWNER and that attitude removed the hardship.

How I pray the words of Jabez, in this moment:

"And Jabez called on the God of Israel, saying, Oh that thou wouldest BLESS ME indeed, and enlarge my coast, and that thine hand might BE WITH ME, and that thou wouldest keep me from evil, that IT MAY NOT GRIEVE ME! And God granted him that which he requested." (1 Chronicles 4:10)

The Hebrew word "grieve" used here means "worry, displease, be sorry"[26] or we'd say "regret." Instead of fighting negative emotions over what we should take joy in, instead of bitterness and a stingy attitude, we become the man Jesus described in Matthew 5:38-42.

---

[26] H6087

"Ye have heard that it hath been said, An eye for an eye, and a tooth for a tooth: But I say unto you, That ye resist not evil: but whosoever shall smite thee on thy right cheek, TURN TO HIM THE OTHER ALSO. And if any man will sue thee at the law, and take away thy coat, LET HIM HAVE THY CLOKE ALSO. And whosoever shall compel thee to go a mile, GO WITH HIM TWAIN. Give to him that asketh thee, and from him that would borrow of thee turn not thou away." (Matthew 5:38-42)

That man, God can use. The GENEROUS HEART of a PASSIONATE member of THE CHURCH will GO into ALL THE WORLD and DO GOOD, stretching out God's hand to HEAL and DELIVER from the OPPRESSION OF THE DEVIL, whether that oppression is mental, physical, or financial.

We are no longer bound to money. It isn't our LOVE.

These are the words of Timothy. *"For the love of money is the root of all evil: which while some coveted after, THEY HAVE ERRED FROM THE FAITH, and pierced themselves through with MANY SORROWS."*[27]

There it is again. With money holding value to us, we will find only SORROW and GRIEF. But what joy abounds the GENEROUS man. Why? Because he or she is just LIKE GOD.

---

[27] 1Ti 6:10

Chapter 13

The Godly Church

Unlike other authors who outline the entire plot of a book and know the beginning, the middle, and the end, I am, what is called amongst writers, a "pantser." This comes from the idea of writing "by the seat of your pants," as the expression goes. I never know more than the scene I am working on. I sometimes have general concept of the storyline, but all the finer details don't come into being until I write them.

I have learned to leave myself notes and to ask questions as I go along. The answers to the questions often help direct the plot. Certain behaviors of men and women, what they would or would not naturally do, help me make choices. Other times, it is more what *could* happen and be believable that would make things more interesting.

I have heard this called "writing in the dark." I am totally in the dark about where things will end up, but I trust my instincts as a writer to get me there.

I was unaware for several years how much this style of writing helped me hear the Holy Spirit. I am never in complete control of what I'm writing. Parts of it are always in limbo. I have the beginning and an idea of the end, but not how to get there. Or I know the middle but can't decide how it will end. It is all a fantastic, fascinating puzzle put together over time.

The words the Holy Spirit speaks to me are much the same. I know they are the Holy Spirit because I have practiced hearing His voice. I cannot write without the INSPIRATION OF GOD. Whether it's fiction or nonfiction. God has to be in it or I'm as blank as a sheet of paper. This is not to say I haven't gotten into my head at times. I have, and every time, I've had to stop and reassess what I'm doing.

I know when the Holy Spirit speaks that if I don't understand it immediately, I will, within time. I write it down in my prayer journal and meditate on it for however long it takes. God always reveals His purpose, but FAITH and PATIENCE are required.

In this manner, this book came to me in stages. I didn't even know it was a book, at first. I was writing "A Good Life" at the time. I assumed it was either for that book or me personally. Sometimes God is simply building me up and teaching me. Yet, over time, all the verses from Acts tied in with what He said about being PASSIONATE, and I understood how they fit together.

He showed me about the destructive power of offense. He gave me the example of the car and its engine over a period of days. My knowledge of automobiles is limited and not a particular interest I have, so that is something I would never have thought of on my own.

I hear because God and I have a relationship developed as I have pressed in, seeking Him above anything else. It started with a need for peace of mind and then became a hunger to know everything. I want all of it! Because the closer to God I am, I become a better person, a better mother, a better wife, a better friend. He shows me where I'm wrong so I can stop acting incorrectly. It makes me stronger and wiser.

I know what to pray about, who to pray for, and what needs my attention in prayer the most. I know when to speak or when to be silent. Which is a lot, I assure you. He helps me out of situations that I would be lost in, on my own power.

I have sought to become the words of 2 Timothy 2:17, *"a man of God throughly furnished unto all good works."* This is the heart of the Bible.

*"All scripture is given by inspiration of God, and is profitable for doctrine, for reproof, for correction, for instruction in righteousness: That the **MAN OF GOD** may be perfect, throughly furnished unto all good works."* (2 Timothy 3:16-17)

God wants a PASSIONATE CHURCH, who desires Him so much that they will set aside all the petty things of the mind and the flesh and seek Him first. I had no choice but to do that. It was either stay weak and afraid or become strong through Christ. My seeking has given me that PASSION. At some point, I stopped caring what other people thought of me for it and began only caring what God thought.

I won't let fear or offense or anger or anything selfish and ungodly stand between me and Him. Not television. I will stop watching. Not music. I will stop listening. Not people. If someone is full of fear and trying to make me afraid, I will distance myself. Remember, we don't have to stand in one place and be tortured? We can let go and walk away.

I can pray and turn the situation over to God. I don't care what my mind is doing, if I'm full of doubts. Or what my body is doing. If my stomach is cramped. I've learned that my mind and my body lie to me. God is truth, and the TRUTH is, I will be fine. God is in control of my life and He supplies all my needs.

HE KEEPS ME THOROUGHLY FURNISHED.

That is the outcome of becoming a PASSIONATE CHILD OF GOD. But as in everything else, where we've studied the positive side, we must also study the negative, and David Guzik's Word Commentary made this so clear.

Using 2 Timothy 3:2-5, He listed the attributes of the ungodly man, the man without God, in the following manner.

> "Men will be lovers of themselves.
> Men will be . . . lovers of money.
> Men will be . . . boasters, proud, blasphemers.
> Men will be . . . disobedient to parents.
> Men will be . . . unthankful, unholy, unloving, unforgiving.
> Men will be . . . slanderers.
> Men will be . . . without self-control.
> Men will be . . . brutal.
> Men will be . . . despisers of good.
> Men will be . . . traitors, headstrong, haughty, lovers of pleasure rather than lovers of God."

These are all characteristics that we are NOT TO BE, and if we had any doubts these are NOT the man of God, this section of verses ends with, *"Having a form of godliness, but DENYING THE POWER thereof: from such [people] turn away."*[1]

Such men have a false godliness. They DENY THE POWER of true godliness and through their denial aren't doing GOOD works but have become despisers of what is GOOD.

We are to become MEN OF GOD, instead.

We don't love money more than God, but we are generous stewards of God's money. It's all His! We aren't boasters of our own efforts, but we highlight what God is doing. We sing His praises.

---

[1] 2Ti 3:5

We are humble, and in our humbleness, we are obedient to authority BECAUSE OF THE ANOINTING ON THE OFFICE. We are thankful for everything in our lives, from the most menial job to the tiny apartment He has provided. We give all praise to God for our success and choose to walk holy lives full of love and the exercise of His love, forgiveness.

We have self-control – of our words and our actions. We don't react. We thoughtfully choose how to respond. We are faithful and gentle and meek.

We love God more than anything else. We are PASSIONATE about Him.

And anytime we slip, if our fire dims because of wrong words and wrong choices, then we turn to the Word of God, which corrects us, showing us the righteous path to walk.

To be "throughly furnished" is to be "complete," to "finish out, equip fully, or accomplish."[2]

It implies continual growth and maturity.

Didn't we read that in Ephesians 5?

"All that he does in us is designed to make us A MATURE CHURCH FOR HIS PLEASURE, until we become A SOURCE OF PRAISE TO HIM—glorious and radiant, beautiful and holy, without fault or flaw." (Ephesians 5:27 TPT)

Denying offense the right to work in us is a sign of maturity. Not speaking critically against government shows maturity. Loving our neighbor through SUBMISSION is maturity.

Not that they can walk all over us, but that their

---

[2] G1822, Strong's Exhaustive Concordance of Hebrews and Greek Words, Thayer's Greek Definitions

actions don't bother us. We are SUBMITTED TO GOD and that brings Him praise. From others, who will notice we are not easily riled, but especially from God. And living in that place of maturity, as radiant and without flaws, as PASSIONATE for our Savior, we will DO GOOD and God HEALS through us. The devil's oppression cannot operate under such conditions.

"With eyes wide open to the mercies of God, I beg you, my brothers, as an act of intelligent worship, to GIVE HIM YOUR BODIES, AS A LIVING SACRIFICE, consecrated to him and acceptable by him. Don't let the world around you squeeze you into its own mould, but let God RE-MOULD YOUR MINDS FROM WITHIN, so that you may prove in practice that the plan of God for you is good, meets all his demands and moves towards THE GOAL OF TRUE MATURITY." (Romans 12:1-2 PHILLIPS)

This is the heart of our obedience. We LIVE through the POWER of the ANOINTING, SUBMITTED to God's will for us. We refuse to become like the world around us, but instead, we think like God.

What does that mean, "think like God?" Relationship. We spend time in His Word, daily, and we meditate on what we've read. Then, we put it into practice. He says to love our neighbor, so when he cuts down the shrubs between our properties, we take a deep breath and let the emotion cool, then we respond with love.

That could mean saying nothing. If you need to speak to him, the Holy Spirit will supply the right time and the correct words to say. Pray about it but continue to PURSUE PEACE.[3] A peaceful, self-controlled person is incredibly

---

[3] Ps 34:14

strong. He is truly MATURE.

"But thou, O MAN OF GOD, flee these things; and follow after righteousness, godliness, faith, love, patience, meekness." (1 Timothy 6:11)

Flee what things? Well, the previous verses list strife, envy, blasphemy, jealousy, conflict, and suspicion. It talks about the love of money being greater than our love for God. It says people who behave these ways *"have been robbed of the truth."*[4]

They are not a MAN OF GOD or a MAN OF TRUTH.

The devil uses PEOPLE to destroy other people. Don't let one of those persons be you.

Be a man or woman of righteousness, a godly person, who is full of FAITH, expectant of SIGNS and WONDERS. A man of God who PREACHES BOLDLY the GOOD NEWS, stretching forth a hand to HEAL, to deliver others from oppression, as Jesus did. Just imagine what God can do through you with your foundation firmly place on His love, His goodness and mercy.[5] His DUNAMIS.

Oh, church, such amazing things! Things far above all that we could ever ask or think.[6]

Stay Filled

John, Jesus' beloved disciple, begins his fantastic revelation of the end of time with a statement that has been mostly overlooked. In chapter 1, verse 10, he writes, *"I was in the Spirit on the Lord's day."*

This is the place and condition he was in when he

---

[4] 1Ti 6:5
[5] Eph 3:17, 9
[6] Eph 3:20

received the vision. He was "in the Spirit" or filled with the Holy Spirit and surrounded by His presence. Such magnificence will not be received otherwise. A man empty and devoid of God will not hear the Spirit's voice. A man of God who is too consumed with his carnal nature will not receive divine revelation.

We must be "in the Spirit."

His amazing revelatory vision came because He was FULL of God.

In Acts 4:8, it says, *"Peter, FILLED with the Holy Ghost, said unto them …"* Peter's boldness, His eloquent words, came from the Holy Spirit because he was FULL.

This thought is repeated in several other places in the Bible.

In Acts 2:1 and 4, we read, *"And when the day of Pentecost was fully come, they were all with one accord in one place … And they were ALL FILLED with the Holy Ghost."* You will recall the filling was loud and heard by those on the street, that it enabled them, men and women, to speak of *"the wonderful works of God,"* in languages they had not learned.[7]

Ephesians 5:18 says, *"And be not drunk with wine, wherein is excess; but BE FILLED with the Spirit,"* equating the supposed pleasure of inebriation as far less than being filled with the Holy Spirit, and in converse to it, damaging.

Reversing to Ephesians 3:19, the apostle Paul prayed that the church *"MIGHT BE FILLED with all the fulness of God."* It is in this fullness that, it says, we will be able to know the size of God's love, and we will walk by faith.

We must STAY FILLED in order to grow and mature so that we can do what God has asked us to do. And by "do" I do not mean simply refusing offense. That is a key to

[7] Act 2:11

"walking" in the Spirit, another way of saying to continually be filled. We "walk" or act according to the Holy Spirit's guidance and under His instructions. We "live" in the Spirit and do not do as our flesh demands.[8]

We stay FULL of the Spirit, so that we can keep up to speed.

What do I mean by that? Well, you will recall our analogy about the car. The engine is DUNAMIS, the power and nature of God, His resources, His might. The fuel is the Holy Spirit. He is what makes the engine run. Faith is the key that cranks it, and the *agape* love of God is the spark.

Offense and criticism, rebellion against government, is like putting diesel fuel in an unleaded engine. It kills it entirely. We can pray and pray and will receive no answers with offense in our hearts.

Prayer is the gas pedal. It is our effort to move the gas to the engine. We pray continually because at no time does a driver let up on the gas and expect to keep going. If you stop pressing the gas pedal, you will come to a halt.

There are two elements missing from this picture, which will complete it.

One, the car is the device that moves us forward. It is how we go from being stagnant in one place, doing our own will, to obeying God and moving in the things of the Spirit. It is us individually, as a member of the body of Christ, and in thinking of the freeway, the church as a whole moving to its destination. All the cars must be traveling in the same direction at the same rate of speed. No one can go backward or drive the wrong direction. If one member slows, then everyone behind him or her will slow.

This is dangerous because the world is an unruly mob, driven by the devil to pursue the church, and when we

---

[8] Gal 5:16, 25

slow, they reach us and begin to whisper untruths, distractions, in our ears. The devil uses PEOPLE as THIEVES AND ROBBERS to derail the church. Suddenly, we're not on the freeway but taking a side trip somewhere that we should not go.

Even worse, sometimes we become deceived enough to open the window or to stop and unlock the door. And in that, there's an important thing to know, the devil cannot force the window open or unlock the door. Only we can allow him in.

There is only one way into the driver's seat – salvation. We get our driver's license by making Jesus Christ Lord of our lives. He is the door, and our praises are the music. If we stay submitted to God and lead holy lives, the devil has no place in the car! He can't even catch us when we're going God's speed.

But that depends entirely on NEVER RUNNING OUT OF GAS. We must stay FULL, our tank topped off at all times. In the natural, that seems impossible, but remember Elijah and the widow at Zarephath?

Elijah had spoken to King Ahab that there would be a drought into the land. He said here would be no rain *"except at his word."*[9]

David Guzik's Word Commentary says of this judgment, "This was a dramatic demonstration against the pagan god Baal, who was thought to be the sky god, the god of the weather. Elijah showed that through his prayers to the God of Israel, Yahweh was mightier than Baal."

How fascinating that is. But there being a drought meant Elijah himself would need to eat. At first, in a miraculous manner, God fed him with meat brought to him by ravens while he lived by a brook. When the brook ran

[9] 1Ki 17:1

dry, he was told to go to Zarephath and look for the widow.

Now, she was desperately poor, the commentaries say. Elijah found her picking up sticks. She hadn't even proper firewood nor anyone to collect it for her. And her statement to him sounds like a serious lack of faith.

"And she said, As the LORD thy God liveth, I have not a cake, but an handful of meal in a barrel, and a little oil in a cruse: and, behold, I am gathering two sticks, that I may go in and dress it for me and my son, that we may eat it, and die." (1 Kings 17:12)

God wants the glory for every miracle. How much more sufficient was it, then, to use a widow who had nothing than to use someone with riches who could afford to pay for it herself? She could say she had no hand in it, except for her actions of faith. This is always God's will. He receives all the praise for the miracles in our lives.[10]

What fear the widow had to obey Elijah's instructions, he removed with his next words.

"And Elijah said unto her, Fear not; go and do as thou hast said: but make me thereof a little cake first, and bring it unto me, and after make for thee and for thy son. For thus saith the LORD God of Israel, The barrel of meal shall not waste, neither shall the cruse of oil fail, until the day that the LORD sendeth rain upon the earth." (1 Kings 17:13-14)

Notice, he said to make him a cake FIRST and THEN to make one for her and her son. He only promised her enough for two cakes! Yet her obedience resulted in enough

---

[10] Rm 9:23 PHILLIPS

to live off of for the entire drought.[11]

I don't believe God kept her small amount of meal to always be a small amount. No, God FILLED her supply and kept it filled. They ate and ate and ate. God is a god of abundance. In 2 Kings 4:1, the prophet Elisha multiplied a widow's small pot of oil into many jars, more than she needed to pay her debts. As much as she could pour, as many vessels as she had to fill, the oil kept multiplying.

What a perfect image of our spiritual lives. **As long as we will pour the Holy Spirit's oil over ourselves, our tanks will stay full, and we will keep moving forward.** Greater, the oil will overflow into the lives of others, and GOD CAN USE US. Because we only STAY FULL by knowing Him, by developing a relationship.

Jesus drew the picture of the Word of God and life in the Spirit as living water. He'd asked a Samaritan woman for a drink and had drawn her into a conversation about the Messiah. Samaritans did not talk to the Jews, which explains her reaction to his request.[12] Jesus had a deeper reason than either controversy or needing a drink, though. He was interested in her heart.

"Jesus replied, 'If you only knew who I am and the gift that God wants to give you—you'd ask me for a drink, and I would give to you LIVING WATER.'

The woman replied, 'But sir, you don't even have a bucket and this well is very deep. So where do you find this 'living water'? Do you really think that you are greater than our ancestor Jacob who dug this well and drank from it himself, along with his children and livestock?'

Jesus answered, 'If you drink from Jacob's well you'll

---

[11] 1Ki 17:15

[12] Jn 4:9

be thirsty again and again, but if anyone drinks the living water I give them, they will never thirst again and will be forever satisfied! For when you drink the water I give you it becomes A GUSHING FOUNTAIN OF THE HOLY SPIRIT, SPRINGING UP AND FLOODING YOU WITH ENDLESS LIFE!'" (John 4:10-14 TPT)

In Him is life and light and wisdom and all we'll ever need to stay on the freeway. If we'll press into the Word of God, make it the center of our days, our tanks will never even fall halfway. But the life of the Holy Spirit is a flood of endless life!

Psalm 23:5 says, *"Thou anointest my head with oil; my cup RUNNETH OVER."* Amos 5:24 in the Voice Translation states, *"Let righteousness flow like a mighty river that NEVER RUNS DRY."* Proverbs 14:27 in the Message Bible says, *"The Fear-of-God is a spring of LIVING water."*

Psalm 1:3 paints a wonderful image of us as healthy, stable trees.

"He will be standing firm like a flourishing tree planted by God's design, deeply rooted by the brooks of bliss, bearing fruit in every season of his life. He is never dry, never fainting, ever blessed, ever prosperous." (TPT)

In reading this psalm, we learn this doesn't happen by chance. We become flourishing trees through our effort. We CHOOSE not to take counsel with the ungodly. We CHOOSE not to stand around with sinners. This doesn't mean we don't minister to the unsaved, but we don't stand and behave like them. We CHOOSE not to sit with scorners, people who CHOOSE OFFENSE over the things of God.

These are our actions done to STAY FULL of the Holy Spirit, not for selfish reasons, but to advance the kingdom of

God. To DO GOOD and HEAL, through DUNAMIS, the will and nature of God.

"And he said unto me, It is done. I am Alpha and Omega, the beginning and the end. I will give unto him that is athirst of the fountain of the water of life freely." (Revelation 21:6)

Why would we stand beside the fountain of LIFE, thirsty, when it is free to take a drink? When it is free to share with other thirsty souls this LIFE-GIVING WATER that HEALS?

The only thing preventing a long-lasting, Spirit-filled move of God in the church is ourselves.

The Passionate Church

In John's revelation are a series of instructions to the seven churches. It is important to notice how he ends each passage with the same series words.

"He that hath an ear, let him hear what the Spirit saith unto the churches."

He that has an ear. I have "an ear." You have "an ear." We are all called to listen to the Holy Spirit's words in these verses. It is not for the labeled ancient cities alone but for everyone in every church. They are the words of the Holy Spirit to reprove, correct, and instruct in righteousness. By heeding these words, we will become men and women of God furnished to all GOOD WORKS.[13]

Next, see that each portion begins with words of praise. Such is our heavenly Father's heart. He doesn't tear

---

[13] 2Ti 3:16

down and destroy; He doesn't condemn. He uplifts and protects. He also brings correction, and each word of praise is followed by a warning with a chance to repent.

We can learn from what they did right. We can see in their behavior, our own. We can also realize where they fell short and correct ourselves. God wasn't sitting blindly in the heavens, while they did what they wanted, but each time, our Lord says, *"I know thy works."* He was paying attention; nothing was hidden from Him.

Jesus said, *"Thy Father, which seeth in secret ..."*[14]

Then in Hebrews 4:13, we read, *"Neither is there any creature that is not manifest in his sight: but all things are naked and opened unto the eyes of him with whom we have to do."*

God sees our GOOD works. He sees where we've worked hard and persevered. None of our efforts to follow Him are in vain or wasted. But also, God knows our faults and flaws. He remembers we are dust.[15] He gave the churches praise, but He also corrected them.

Two of these warnings ring loudly in my ears.

To Ephesus, He said:

"But I have this against you: you have abandoned THE PASSIONATE LOVE you had for me at the beginning." (Revelation 2:4 TPT)

An un-passionate church is one consumed with rules and regulations, with their personal lives, and the world around them. Ephesus had withstood trials and persecutions. They'd taken a strong stand against evil, but their PASSION was gone. Church had become an hour on

---

[14] Mk 16:18

[15] Ps 103:14

Sunday and nothing more. Like a junk yard full of cars without engines, there was nothing to crank, no engine, and no fuel. You can have the keys but, put them in the ignition of a car without an engine, and you're going nowhere.

Now, read the Holy Spirit's words to Laodicea. They were in even worse shape. Unable to see past the pole in their own eye,[16] instead of equipping the saints, they were full of pride and judgment.

"I know all that you do, and I know that you are neither FROZEN IN APATHY nor FERVENT WITH PASSION. How I wish you were either one or the other! But because you are neither cold nor hot, but lukewarm, I am about to spit you from my mouth. For you claim, 'I'm rich and getting richer—I don't need a thing.' Yet you are clueless that you're miserable, poor, blind, barren, and naked!" (Revelation 3:15-17 TPT)

The King James Version uses the term "lukewarm."

Here is a church grown tepid. They think not of helping others but are deluded by their opinion of themselves. **They think they are well-dressed when, in fact, they are naked and miserable, walking around in circles.** They've been deceived into believing it's okay to stand with one leg on either side of the fence. But their resistance to the things of the Holy Spirit, their lack of growth, is open and exposed to God. And He pleads with them to repent, to cover themselves, and hear His words of correction. Not in anger but out of love.

This is true correction.

"All those I dearly love I unmask and train. So repent

[16] Mt 7:3-4

and BE EAGER to pursue what is right," the Holy Spirit says.[17]

God's correction is always done out of love. For that matter, His desire for a PASSIONATE church is so He can show His love to the entire world—love that SAVES and HEALS and DELIVERS from demonic oppression.

Here's the good news: God is longsuffering. Try and count the number of times He forgave Israel in the Old Testament. They are innumerable and span thousands of years! Again and again, they sinned. Again and again, He showed mercy.

God desires repentance. He longs to forgive. What the Ephesian church had lost, what Laodicea had set aside, their hearts could be reignited, their fervor stirred up, and the rewards of that were exceedingly rich.

"Behold, I'm standing at the door, knocking. If your heart is open to hear my voice and you open the door within, I will come in to you and feast with you, and you will feast with me. And to the one who conquers I will give the privilege of sitting with me on my throne, just as I conquered and sat down with my Father on his throne." (Revelation 3:20-21)

God isn't asking us to crawl toward him through the dust, suffering for our behavior. He is tender and gentle, though stern. He will feed us and strengthen us where we are at. He'll walk with us until we're able to go on our own. He only asks sincere willingness, and He will revive us once again.

"Revive us, O God! Let your beaming face shine upon us with the sunrise rays of glory; then nothing will be able to

---

[17] Rev 3:19 TPT

stop us." (Psalm 80:3 TPT)

Nothing can stop us when we are united with Him. No enemy can stand against us.[18]

We are the triumphant church!

We live and move and have our being in Him once more.[19] Filled with His Spirit, we are CONSUMED with Him. Our passion reignited, we cannot help but extol His praises.

"You are my strength and my shield from every danger. When I fully trust in you, help is on the way. I jump for joy and burst forth with ECSTATIC, PASSIONATE PRAISE! I will sing songs of what you mean to me!" (Psalm 28:7 TPT)

He is better than any sports team in that winning moment, trophy in hand, fans jumping for joy. Far, far better than that!

Because the God of the universe, the Creator of life, has poured His NATURE into us. We are CHRISTIANS, His ANOINTED children, filled with His EXCELLENCE and His MIGHT. We are sent to do GREATER WORKS. We stand in the POWER of the Holy Spirit, BOLDLY, like the church of Acts, unafraid.

"And when they had prayed, the place was shaken where they were assembled together; and they were all filled with the Holy Ghost, and they spake the word of God with boldness." (Acts 4:29-31)

This is THE CHURCH.

A people not weakened by the desires of the flesh or

---

[18] Jos 1:5

[19] Act 17:28

the offenses of the darkened world, not slowed by any of the devil's distractions, nor afraid of the will of men, but our hearts in tune with Almighty God, we will GO FORTH and SIGNS and WONDERS will follow.

A church of the miraculous. A PASSIONATE CHURCH, standing firm in the ANOINTING, whatever we may face, until the end of time.

For Study

The Scriptures are to help us mature and be like Christ.

"All scripture is given by inspiration of God, and is profitable for doctrine, for reproof, for correction, for instruction in righteousness." (2 Timothy 3:16)

"All scripture is inspired by God and is useful for teaching the faith and correcting error, for re-setting the direction of a man's life and training him in good living. The scriptures are the comprehensive equipment of the man of God and fit him fully for all branches of his work." (2 Timothy 3:16-17 PHILLIPS)

"As newborn babes, desire the sincere milk of the word, that ye may grow thereby." (1 Peter 2:2)

Jesus was ANOINTED with POWER to DO GOOD and HEAL those OPPRESSED OF THE DEVIL.

"How God ANOINTED Jesus of Nazareth with the Holy Ghost and with POWER (DUNAMIS): who went about DOING GOOD, and HEALING all that were OPPRESSED OF THE DEVIL; for GOD WAS WITH HIM." (Acts 10:38)

"Yet he was the one who carried OUR SICKNESSES and endured the torment OF OUR SUFFERINGS. We viewed him as one who was being punished for something he himself had done, as one who was struck down by God and brought low. But it was because of our rebellious deeds that he was pierced and because of our sins that he was crushed. He

endured the punishment that made us COMPLETELY WHOLE, and in his wounding WE FOUND OUR HEALING." (Isaiah 53:4-5 TPT)

"And so Jesus went throughout Galilee. He taught in the synagogues. He preached the GOOD NEWS of the Kingdom, and He HEALED people, RIDDING THEIR BODIES OF SICKNESS AND DISEASE. Word spread all over Syria, as more and more sick people came to Him. The innumerable ill who came before Him had all sorts of diseases, they were in crippling pain; they were possessed by demons; they had seizures; they were paralyzed. BUT JESUS HEALED THEM ALL." (Matthew 4:23-24 VOICE)

"Jesus went through many towns and villages. He taught in their synagogues. He preached the good news of the kingdom of God. HE HEALED EVERY DISEASE AND SICKNESS." (Matthew 9:35 VOICE)

"Though Jesus wanted solitude, when He saw the crowds, He had compassion on them, and HE HEALED the sick and the lame." (Matthew 14:14 VOICE)

"Crowds thronged to Him there, bringing the lame, the maimed, the blind, the crippled, the mute, and many other sick and broken people. They laid them at His feet, AND HE HEALED THEM." (Matthew 15:30 VOICE)

"The beginning of the gospel [GOOD NEWS] of Jesus Christ, the Son of God." (Mark 1:1)

"For HE HAD HEALED MANY; insomuch that they pressed upon him for to touch him, as many as had plagues. And unclean spirits, when they saw him, fell down before him,

and cried, saying, Thou art the Son of God." (Mark 3:10-11)

"And when he had opened the book, he found the place where it was written, The SPIRIT OF THE LORD is upon me, because he hath ANOINTED me to preach THE GOSPEL to the poor; he hath sent me TO HEAL the brokenhearted, to PREACH DELIVERANCE to the captives, and RECOVERING OF SIGHT to the blind, to SET AT LIBERTY them that are bruised, To preach the acceptable year of the Lord. And he closed the book, and he gave it again to the minister, and sat down. And the eyes of all them that were in the synagogue were fastened on him. And he began to say unto them, This day is this scripture fulfilled in your ears." (Luke 4:17-21)

"And the whole multitude sought to touch him: for there went VIRTUE [DUNAMIS] out of him, and healed them all." (Luke 6:19)

"For God sent not his Son into the world to condemn the world; but that the world through him MIGHT BE SAVED [SOZO]." (John 3:17)

"And I [Saul] said, Who art thou, Lord? And he said, I am Jesus whom thou persecutest. But rise, and stand upon thy feet: for I have appeared unto thee for this purpose, to make thee a minister and a witness both of these things which thou hast seen, and of those things in the which I will appear unto thee; Delivering thee from the people, and from the Gentiles, unto whom now I send thee, To open their eyes, and TO TURN THEM FROM DARKNESS TO LIGHT, AND FROM THE POWER OF SATAN UNTO GOD, that they may RECEIVE FORGIVENESS of sins, and inheritance among them which are sanctified by faith that is in me." (Acts 26:15-18)

"FOR THIS PURPOSE the Son of God was manifested, that he might DESTROY THE WORKS OF THE DEVIL." (1 John 3:8)

Dunamis (Holy Ghost) power is:

"Inherent power, power residing in a thing by virtue of its nature, or which a person or thing exerts and puts forth; moral power and excellence of soul; the power and influence which belong to riches and wealth; power and resources arising from numbers; power consisting in or resting upon armies, forces, hosts." (G2411, Thayer's Greek Definitions, www.e-sword.net)

SOZO (Salvation) is:

To "save, deliver, protect, heal, preserve, make whole." (G4982, Strong's Hebrew and Greek Dictionaries, www.e-sword.net)

The POWERFUL Word of God

"He saith unto them, But whom say ye that I am? And Simon Peter answered and said, Thou art THE CHRIST, the Son of the living God. And Jesus answered and said unto him, Blessed art thou, Simon Barjona: for flesh and blood hath not revealed it unto thee, but my Father which is in heaven. And I say also unto thee, That thou art Peter, and UPON THIS ROCK [of revelation that Jesus was the Christ] I will build my church; and the gates of hell shall not prevail against it." (Matthew 16:15-18)

"I give you the name Peter, a stone. AND THIS TRUTH OF WHO I AM will be the bedrock foundation on which I will build my church—my legislative assembly, and the power of

death will not be able to overpower it!" [Matthew 16:18 TPT)

"The church will reign triumphant even at the gates of hell." (Matthew 16:18 VOICE)

"And the angel answered and said unto her, The HOLY GHOST SHALL COME UPON THEE, and the POWER [DUNAMIS] of the Highest shall overshadow thee: therefore also that holy thing which shall be born of thee shall be called THE SON OF GOD. And, behold, thy cousin Elisabeth, she hath also conceived a son in her old age: and this is the sixth month with her, who was called barren. FOR WITH GOD NOTHING SHALL BE IMPOSSIBLE." (Luke 1:35-37)

"The statement [from Luke 1:37] is, Every (πᾶν) word of God shall not (οὐκ) be powerless." (Vincent's Word Studies, www.e-sword.net)

We are to GO and DO like Christ.

"Jesus called His twelve disciples to Him. He endowed them with THE AUTHORITY to heal sickness and disease and to drive demons out of those who were possessed." (Matthew 10:1 VOICE)

"And as ye GO, preach, saying, the kingdom of heaven is at hand. heal the sick, cleanse the lepers, raise the dead, cast out devils: freely ye have received, freely give." (Matthew 10:7-8 VOICE)

"And THESE SIGNS shall follow them that believe; IN MY NAME shall they cast out devils; they shall speak with new tongues; They shall take up serpents; and if they drink any

deadly thing, it shall not hurt them; they shall lay hands on the sick, and they SHALL RECOVER." (Mark 16:17-18)

"After these things the Lord appointed other seventy also, AND SENT them two and two before his face into every city and place, whither he himself would come ... AND HEAL the sick that are therein, and say unto them, The kingdom of God is come nigh unto you." (Luke 10:1, 9)

"And the seventy returned again with joy, saying, Lord, even the devils are subject unto us through thy name." (Luke 10:17)

"I beheld Satan as lightning fall from heaven. Behold, I give unto you POWER [AUTHORITY] to tread on serpents and scorpions, and over all the power of the enemy: and nothing shall by any means hurt you. Notwithstanding in this rejoice not, that the spirits are subject unto you; but rather rejoice, because your names are written in heaven." (Luke 10:18-20)

"Which now of these three, thinkest thou, was neighbour unto him that fell among the thieves? And he said, He that shewed mercy on him. Then said Jesus unto him, GO, AND DO thou likewise." (Luke 10:36-37)

"And fear came upon every soul: and many WONDERS and SIGNS were done BY THE APOSTLES." (Act 2:43)

"Rulers and elders of the people, yesterday A GOOD DEED was done. Someone who WAS SICK WAS HEALED. If you're asking us how this happened, I want all of you and all of the people of Israel to know this man standing in front of you—obviously in good health—was HEALED BY THE AUTHORITY OF JESUS OF NAZARETH, THE ANOINTED ONE. This is the

same Jesus whom you crucified and whom God raised from the dead. He is 'the stone that you builders rejected who has become the very stone that holds together the entire foundation' on which a new temple is being built. There is no one else who can rescue us, and there is NO OTHER NAME UNDER HEAVEN given to any human BY WHOM WE MAY BE RESCUED." (Acts 4:8-13 VOICE)

"And he gave some, apostles; and some, prophets; and some, evangelists; and some, pastors and teachers; For the perfecting of the saints, FOR THE WORK OF THE MINISTRY, for the edifying of the body of Christ." (Ephesians 4:11-12)

"Therefore to him that KNOWETH TO DO GOOD, AND DOETH IT NOT, to him IT IS SIN." (James 4:17)

We will do GREATER WORKS (in quantity).

"I tell you the truth: whoever believes in Me will be able to do what I have done, BUT THEY WILL DO EVEN GREATER THINGS, because I will return to be with the Father. Whatever you ask for in My name, I will do it so that the Father will get glory from the Son. Let Me say it again: if you ask for anything in My name, I will do it." (John 14:12-14 VOICE)

"Verily, verily, I say unto you, He that believeth on me, THE WORKS THAT I DO SHALL HE DO ALSO; and GREATER WORKS THAN THESE SHALL HE DO; because I go unto my Father." (John 14:12)

We (the church) are partners with God's nature.

"Everything we could ever need for life and complete devotion to God has already been deposited in us BY HIS DIVINE POWER. For all this was lavished upon us through the rich experience of knowing him who has called us by name and invited us to come to him through a glorious manifestation of his goodness. As a result of this, he has given you magnificent promises that are beyond all price, so that through the power of these tremendous promises YOU CAN EXPERIENCE PARTNERSHIP WITH THE DIVINE NATURE, by which you have escaped the corrupt desires that are of the world." (2 Peter 1:3-4 TPT)

The Holy Spirit is our teacher (comforter) and advocate.

"If ye love me, keep my commandments. And I will pray the Father, and he shall give you ANOTHER COMFORTER, that he may abide with you for ever; Even THE SPIRIT OF TRUTH; whom the world cannot receive, because it seeth him not, neither knoweth him: but ye know him; FOR HE DWELLETH WITH YOU, AND SHALL BE IN YOU. I will not leave you comfortless: I WILL COME TO YOU." (John 14:15-18)

"But ye shall receive POWER, after that the Holy Ghost is come upon you: and ye shall be witnesses unto me both in Jerusalem, and in all Judaea, and in Samaria, and unto the uttermost part of the earth." (Acts 1:8)

"Repent, and be baptized every one of you in the name of Jesus Christ for the remission of sins, and YE SHALL RECEIVE the gift of the Holy Ghost. FOR THE PROMISE IS UNTO YOU, AND TO YOUR CHILDREN, AND TO ALL THAT ARE AFAR OFF, even as many as the Lord our God shall call." (Act 2:38-39)

We can do ALL THINGS through the Holy Spirit.

"But the Comforter, which is the Holy Ghost, whom the Father will send in my name, he shall teach you ALL THINGS, and bring ALL THINGS to your remembrance, whatsoever I have said unto you." (John 14:26)

"What shall we then say to these things? If God be for us, who can be against us? He that spared not his own Son, but delivered him up for us all, how shall he not with him also freely give us ALL THINGS?" (Romans 8:31-32)

"And God is able to make ALL grace abound toward you; that ye, ALWAYS having ALL SUFFICIENCY in ALL THINGS, may abound to EVERY good work." (2 Corinthians 9:8)

"I can do ALL THINGS through Christ which strengtheneth me." (Philippians 4:13)

"And the Lord give thee understanding in ALL THINGS." (2 Timothy 1:7)

"According as his divine power hath given unto us ALL THINGS that pertain unto life and godliness, through the knowledge of him that hath called us to glory and virtue." (2 Peter 1:3)

We are the PASSIONATE church. We are not apathetic (lukewarm).

"The realm of heaven's kingdom is bursting forth, and PASSIONATE PEOPLE have taken hold of its POWER." (Matthew 11:11 TPT)

"You are my strength and my shield from every danger. When I fully trust in you, help is on the way. I jump for joy and burst forth with ECSTATIC, PASSIONATE PRAISE! I will sing songs of what you mean to me!" (Psalm 28:7 TPT)

"Fasten me upon your heart as a seal of fire forevermore. This living, consuming flame will seal you as my prisoner of love. MY PASSION IS STRONGER than the chains of death and the grave, ALL CONSUMING as the very flashes of fire from the burning heart of God. Place this fierce, unrelenting fire over your entire being." (Song of Solomon 8:6 TPT)

"But when I tell myself, I'll never mention Your name or speak for You again, it's no use. The word of God burns in my heart; IT IS LIKE FIRE in my bones. I try to hold it all in, but I cannot." (Jeremiah 20:9 VOICE)

"And his disciples remembered that it was written, THE ZEAL of thine house hath eaten me up." (John 2:17)

"But I have this against you: you have abandoned THE PASSIONATE LOVE you had for me at the beginning." (Revelation 2:4 TPT)

"I know all that you do, and I know that you are neither FROZEN IN APATHY nor FERVENT WITH PASSION. How I wish you were either one or the other! But because you are neither cold nor hot, but lukewarm, I am about to spit you from my mouth. For you claim, 'I'm rich and getting richer—I don't need a thing.' Yet you are clueless that you're miserable, poor, blind, barren, and naked!" (Revelation 3:15-17 TPT)

We are a MATURE church. We ARE NOT carnal and full of strife.

"With eyes wide open to the mercies of God, I beg you, my brothers, as an act of intelligent worship, to give him your bodies, as a living sacrifice, consecrated to him and acceptable by him. Don't let the world around you squeeze you into its own mould, but let God re-mould your minds from within, so that you may prove in practice that the plan of God for you is good, meets all his demands and moves towards THE GOAL OF TRUE MATURITY." (Romans 12:1-2 PHILLIPS)

"And to the husbands, you are to demonstrate love for your wives with the same tender devotion that Christ demonstrated to us, his bride. For he died for us, sacrificing himself to make us holy and pure, cleansing us through the showering of the pure water of the Word of God. All that he does in us is designed to make us A MATURE CHURCH FOR HIS PLEASURE, until we become A SOURCE OF PRAISE TO HIM—glorious and radiant, beautiful and holy, without fault or flaw." (Ephesians 5:25-27 TPT)

"And I, brethren, could not speak unto you as unto spiritual, but as unto carnal, even as unto babes in Christ. I have fed you with milk, and not with meat: for hitherto ye were not able to bear it, neither yet now are ye able. For ye are yet carnal: for whereas there is among you envying, and strife, and divisions, are ye not carnal, and walk as men?" (1 Corinthians 3:1-3)

We are an EARNEST (fervent) church.

"REVIVE us, O God! Let your beaming face shine upon us with the sunrise rays of glory; then nothing will be able to stop us." (Psalm 80:3 TPT)

"Confess your faults one to another, and pray one for another, that ye may be healed. The EFFECTUAL FERVENT PRAYER of a righteous man availeth much." (James 5:16)

"Beloved, when I gave all diligence to write unto you of the common salvation, it was needful for me to write unto you, and exhort you that ye should EARNESTLY CONTEND for the faith which was once delivered unto the saints." (Jude 1:3)

"All those I dearly love I unmask and train. So repent and BE EAGER to pursue what is right," the Holy Spirit says. (Revelation 3:19 TPT)

We are a BOLD church.

"And now, Lord, behold their threatenings: and grant unto thy servants, that with ALL BOLDNESS they may speak thy word, BY STRETCHING FORTH THINE HAND TO HEAL; and that SIGNS AND WONDERS MAY BE DONE by the name of thy holy child Jesus." (Acts 4:29-30)

"Praying always with all prayer and supplication in the Spirit, and watching thereunto with all perseverance and supplication for all saints; And for me, that utterance may be given unto me, that I may open my mouth BOLDLY, to make known the mystery of the gospel, For which I am an ambassador in bonds: that therein I may SPEAK BOLDLY, as I ought to speak." (Ephesians 6:18-20)

"Let us therefore COME BOLDLY unto the throne of grace, that we may obtain mercy, and find grace to help in time of need." (Hebrews 4:16)

We are the FORGIVING church. We DO NOT condemn anyone.

"For if ye FORGIVE men their trespasses, your heavenly Father will also forgive you: But if ye FORGIVE NOT men their trespasses, neither will your Father forgive your trespasses." (Matthew 6:14-15)

"Therefore I say unto you, What things soever ye desire, when ye pray, believe that ye receive them, and ye shall have them. And WHEN YE STAND PRAYING, FORGIVE, if ye have ought against any: that your Father also which is in heaven may forgive you your trespasses. But IF YE DO NOT FORGIVE, neither will your Father which is in heaven forgive your trespasses." (Mark 11:24-26)

"And I [Saul] said, Who art thou, Lord? And he said, I am Jesus whom thou persecutest. But rise, and stand upon thy feet: for I have appeared unto thee for this purpose, to make thee a minister and a witness both of these things which thou hast seen, and of those things in the which I will appear unto thee; Delivering thee from the people, and from the Gentiles, unto whom now I send thee, To open their eyes, and to turn them from darkness to light, and from the power of Satan unto God, that they may RECEIVE FORGIVENESS of sins, and inheritance among them which are sanctified by faith that is in me." (Acts 26:15-18)

"There is therefore now NO CONDEMNATION to them which are in Christ Jesus, who walk not after the flesh, but after the Spirit." (Romans 8:1)

We are the LOVING church.

"But I say unto you, LOVE YOUR ENEMIES, bless them that curse you, do good to them that hate you, and pray for them which despitefully use you, and persecute you; that ye may be the children of your Father which is in heaven: for he maketh his sun to rise on the evil and on the good, and sendeth rain on the just and on the unjust." (Matthew 5:44-45)

"A new commandment I give unto you, That ye LOVE ONE ANOTHER; as I have loved you, that ye also LOVE ONE ANOTHER." (John 13:34)

"This is my commandment, That ye LOVE ONE ANOTHER, as I have loved you." (John 15:12)

"Don't owe anyone anything, with the exception of LOVE TO ONE ANOTHER—that is a debt which never ends—because the person who loves others has fulfilled the law." (Romans 13:8 VOICE)

"Therefore if thine enemy hunger, feed him; if he thirst, give him drink: for in so doing thou shalt heap coals of fire on his head. Be not overcome of evil, but overcome evil WITH GOOD." (Romans 12:20-21)

"Though I speak with the tongues of men and of angels, and have not charity, I am become as sounding brass, or a tinkling cymbal. And though I have the gift of prophecy, and

understand all mysteries, and all knowledge; and though I have all faith, so that I could remove mountains, AND HAVE NOT CHARITY, I AM NOTHING. And though I bestow all my goods to feed the poor, and though I give my body to be burned, and HAVE NOT CHARITY, IT PROFITETH ME NOTHING." (1 Corinthians 13:1-3)

"Until then, there are three things that remain: faith, hope, and love—yet LOVE SURPASSES THEM ALL." (1 Corinthians 13:13 TPT)

"For in Jesus Christ neither circumcision availeth any thing, nor uncircumcision; but faith which WORKETH BY LOVE." (Galatians 5:6)

"Beloved, let us LOVE ONE ANOTHER: for love is of God; and every one that loveth is born of God, and knoweth God." (1 John 4:7)

We (the church) DO NOT take offense. Offense kills the power of God. It is unbelief.

"Jesus answered and said unto them, Go and shew John again those things which ye do hear and see: The blind receive their sight, and the lame walk, the lepers are cleansed, and the deaf hear, the dead are raised up, and the poor have the gospel preached to them. And blessed is he, WHOSOEVER SHALL NOT BE OFFENDED IN ME." (Matthew 11:4-6)

"From whence hath this man these things? and what wisdom is this which is given unto him, that even such mighty works are wrought by his hands? Is not this the carpenter, the son of Mary, the brother of James, and Joses,

and of Juda, and Simon? and are not his sisters here with us? AND THEY WERE OFFENDED AT HIM. But Jesus said unto them, A prophet is not without honour, but in his own country, and among his own kin, and in his own house. AND HE COULD THERE DO NO MIGHTY WORK [DUNAMIS], save that he laid his hands upon a few sick folk, and healed them. And he marvelled because of their UNBELIEF." (Mark 6:2-6)

We (the church) DO NOT cause offense.

"Wherefore, if meat make my brother to offend, I will eat no flesh while the world standeth, lest I make my brother to offend." (1 Corinthians 8:13)

"So if any type of food is an issue that causes my brothers and sisters to fall away from God, then God forbid I should ever eat it again so that I would NEVER BE THE CRACK, THE RISE, or THE ROCK ON THE ROAD that CAUSES THEM TO STUMBLE." (1 Corinthians 8:13 VOICE)

"Be gentle and humble, UNOFFENDABLE in your patience with others." (Colossians 3:12 TPT)

We (the church) DO NOT hold judgment.

"Don't pick on people, jump on their failures, criticize their faults— unless, of course, you want the same treatment. That critical spirit has a way of boomeranging." (Matthew 7:1 MSG)

"Refuse to be a critic full of bias toward others, and judgment will not be passed on you." (Matthew 7:1 TPT)

"JUDGE NOT, that ye be not judged. For with what judgment

ye judge, ye shall be judged: and with what measure ye mete, it shall be measured to you again. And why beholdest thou the mote that is in thy brother's eye, but considerest not the beam that is in thine own eye? Or how wilt thou say to thy brother, Let me pull out the mote out of thine eye; and, behold, a beam is in thine own eye? Thou hypocrite, first cast out the beam out of thine own eye; and then shalt thou see clearly to cast out the mote out of thy brother's eye." (Matthew 7:1-5)

"He that is without sin among you, let him first cast a stone at her." (John 8:7)

"We must resolve NEVER TO JUDGE others and never to place an obstacle or impediment in their paths that could cause them to trip and fall." (Romans 14:13 VOICE)

We (the church) are NOT "thieves and robbers" of another man's blessing.

"And said unto them, It is written, My house shall be called the house of prayer; but ye have made it a DEN OF THIEVES." (Matthew 21:13)

"Then said Jesus unto them again, Verily, verily, I say unto you, I am the door of the sheep. all that ever came before me are THIEVES AND ROBBERS: but the sheep did not hear them. I am the door: by me if any man enter in, he shall be saved, and shall go in and out, and find pasture. THE THIEF COMETH NOT, BUT FOR TO STEAL, AND TO KILL, AND TO DESTROY: I am come that they might have life, and that they might have it more abundantly." (John 10:7-10)

"Finally, be ye all of one mind, having compassion one of another, love as brethren, be pitiful, be courteous: Not rendering evil for evil, or railing for railing: but CONTRARIWISE BLESSING; knowing that ye are thereunto called, that ye should inherit a blessing." (1 Peter 3:8-9)

"Finally, all of you, be like-minded and show sympathy, love, compassion, and humility to and for each other—not paying back evil with evil or insult with insult, but REPAYING THE BAD WITH A BLESSING. It was this you were called to do, so that you might inherit a blessing." (1 Peter 3:8-9 VOICE)

We are the SERVING church.

"If I then, your Lord and Master, have washed your feet; YE ALSO OUGHT TO WASH ONE ANOTHER'S FEET. For I have given you an example, that YE SHOULD DO AS I HAVE DONE to you. Verily, verily, I say unto you, The servant is not greater than his lord; neither he that is sent greater than he that sent him." (John 13:14-16)

"For though I be free from all men, yet have I made MYSELF SERVANT UNTO ALL, that I might gain the more." (1 Corinthians 9:19)

"Let this mind be in you, which was also in Christ Jesus: Who, being in the form of God, thought it not robbery to be equal with God: But made himself of no reputation, and TOOK UPON HIM THE FORM OF A SERVANT, and was made in the likeness of men: And being found in fashion as a man, HE HUMBLED HIMSELF, and became obedient unto death, even the death of the cross." (Philippians 2:5-8)

We are the SUBMISSIVE church.

"For wives, this means being supportive to your husbands like you are tenderly devoted to our Lord, for the husband provides leadership for the wife, just as Christ provides leadership for his church, as the Savior and Reviver of the body. In the same way the church is devoted to Christ, let the wives be devoted to their husbands in everything. And to the husbands, you are to demonstrate love for your wives with the same tender devotion that Christ demonstrated to us, his bride. For he died for us, sacrificing himself to make us holy and pure, cleansing us through the showering of the pure water of the Word of God." (Ephesians 5:22-26 TPT)

"Obey them that have the rule over you, AND SUBMIT yourselves: for they watch for your souls, as they that must give account, that they may do it with joy, and not with grief: for that is unprofitable for you." (Hebrews 13:17)

"SUBMIT YOURSELVES THEREFORE TO GOD. Resist the devil, and he will flee from you." (James 4:7)

"Likewise, ye younger, SUBMIT YOURSELVES unto the elder. Yea, ALL OF YOU BE SUBJECT ONE TO ANOTHER, and be clothed with humility: for God resisteth the proud, and giveth grace to the humble." (1 Peter 5:5)

We (the church) YIELD to the Holy Spirit's discipline. It is to our benefit.

"A true athlete will be disciplined in every respect, practicing constant self-control in order to win a laurel wreath that quickly withers. But we run our race to win a victor's crown that will last forever." (1 Corinthians 9:15 TPT)

"Now all discipline seems to be more pain than pleasure at the time, yet later it will produce a transformation of character, bringing a harvest of righteousness and peace to those WHO YIELD to it." (Hebrews 12:11 TPT)

We are a church of INTEGRITY. God knows our heart (motives).

"But the LORD said unto Samuel, Look not on his countenance, or on the height of his stature; because I have refused him: for the LORD seeth not as man seeth; for man looketh on the outward appearance, BUT THE LORD LOOKETH ON THE HEART." (1 Samuel 16:7)

"Shall not God search this out? for HE KNOWETH THE SECRETS OF THE HEART." (Psalms 44:21)

"We are all in love with our own opinions, convinced they're correct. But the Lord is in the midst of us, testing and probing OUR EVERY MOTIVE." (Proverbs 16:2 TPT)

"That thine alms may be in secret: and thy Father WHICH SEETH IN SECRET himself shall reward thee openly." (Matthew 6:4)

"You ignore the most important duty of all: to walk in the love of God, to display mercy to others, and to LIVE WITH INTEGRITY." (Matthew 23:23 TPT)

"For if our heart condemn us, God is greater than our heart, and KNOWETH ALL THINGS." (1 John 3:20)

We (the church) are NOT to be HYPOCRITES (false humility).

"How could you say to your friend, 'Let me show you where you're wrong,' when you're guilty of even more? You're being hypercritical and a hypocrite!" (Matthew 7:4-5 TPT)

"Outwardly you masquerade AS RIGHTEOUS people, but inside your hearts you are FULL OF HYPOCRISY and lawlessness." (Matthew 23:28 TPT)

"But the wisdom that is from above is first pure, then peaceable, gentle, and easy to be intreated, full of mercy and good fruits, without partiality, and WITHOUT HYPOCRISY. And the fruit of righteousness is sown in peace of them that make peace." (James 3:17-18)

We (the church) BUILD OTHERS UP. We ENCOURAGE them with our words.

"And so the good man (who is filled with goodness) speaks good words, while the evil man (who is filled with evil) speaks evil words. I tell you this: on the day of judgment, people will be called to account FOR EVERY CARELESS WORD they have ever said." (Matthew 12:35-36 VOICE)

"Therefore, as a witness of the Lord, I insist on this: that you no longer walk in the outsiders' ways—with minds devoted to worthless pursuits ... But this is not the path of the Anointed One, which you have learned ... so put away your lies and speak the truth to one another because we are all part of one another. When you are angry, don't let it carry you into sin. Don't let the sun set with anger in your heart OR GIVE THE DEVIL ROOM TO WORK. ... Don't let EVEN ONE

ROTTEN WORD SEEP OUT OF YOUR MOUTHS. Instead, offer only fresh words THAT BUILD OTHERS UP when they need it most. That way your good words will COMMUNICATE GRACE to those who hear them." (Ephesians 3:17, 20, 25-27, 29 VOICE)

We LIVE IN HARMONY with others.

"LIVE IN HARMONY with each other. Don't become snobbish but take a real interest in ordinary people. Don't become set in your own opinions." (Romans 12:16 PHILLIPS)

"Live happily together in A SPIRIT OF HARMONY, and be as mindful of another's worth as you are your own. Don't live with a lofty mind-set, thinking you are too important to serve others, but be willing to do menial tasks and identify with those who are humble minded. Don't be smug or even think for a moment that you know it all." (Romans 12:16 TPT)

We (the church) RELY ON GOD, not our opinions.

"Trust in the Lord completely, and DO NOT RELY ON YOUR OWN OPINIONS. With all your heart rely on him to guide you, and he will lead you in every decision you make." (Proverbs 3:5 TPT)

"There's only one thing worse than a fool, and that's the smug, conceited man ALWAYS IN LOVE WITH HIS OWN OPINIONS." (Proverbs 26:14 TPT)

"Open your heart and consider my words. WATCH OUT THAT YOU DO NOT MISTAKE YOUR OPINIONS for revelation-light!" (Luke 11:35 TPT)

We are the COMPASSIONATE church.

"Howbeit Jesus suffered him not, but saith unto him, Go home to thy friends, and tell them how great things the Lord hath done for thee, and hath HAD COMPASSION on thee." (Mark 5:19)

"BANISH bitterness, rage and anger, shouting and slander, and ANY AND ALL MALICIOUS THOUGHTS—these are poison. INSTEAD, be kind and compassionate. Graciously forgive one another just as God has forgiven you through the Anointed, our Liberating King." (Ephesians 4:31-32 VOICE)

"Hereby perceive we the love of God, because he laid down his life for us: and we ought to lay down our lives for the brethren. But whoso hath this world's good, and seeth his brother have need, and shutteth up his bowels of COMPASSION from him, how dwelleth the love of God in him?" (1 John 3:16-17)

We (the church) NEVER DISCRIMINATE against anyone for any reason.

"For there is NO DIFFERENCE between the Jew and the Greek: for the same Lord over all is rich unto all that call upon him." (Romans 10:12)

"There is neither Jew nor Greek, there is neither bond nor free, there is neither male nor female: for ye ARE ALL ONE in Christ Jesus." (Galatians 3:28)

"Where there is neither Greek nor Jew, circumcision nor uncircumcision, Barbarian, Scythian, bond nor free: but CHRIST IS ALL, AND IN ALL." (Colossians 3:11)

"My dear brothers and sisters, how can you claim to have faith in our glorious Lord Jesus Christ if you favor some people over others? ... If you give special attention and a good seat to the rich person, but you say to the poor one, "You can stand over there, or else sit on the floor"—well, doesn't this DISCRIMINATION show that your judgments are guided by evil motives?" (James 2:1, 3 NLT)

"But the wisdom that is from above is first pure, then peaceable, gentle, and easy to be intreated, full of mercy and good fruits, WITHOUT PARTIALITY, and without hypocrisy. And the fruit of righteousness is sown in peace of them that make peace." (James 3:17-18)

We are the PATIENT church.

"WAIT ON THE LORD, and keep his way, and he shall exalt thee to inherit the land: when the wicked are cut off, thou shalt see it." (Psalms 37:34)

"In your PATIENCE possess ye your souls." (Luke 21:19)

"But that's not all! Even in times of trouble we have a joyful confidence, knowing that our pressures will develop in us PATIENT ENDURANCE. And patient endurance will refine our character, and proven character leads us back to hope." (Romans 5:3-4 TPT)

"My brethren, count it all joy when ye fall into divers temptations; Knowing this, that the trying of your faith WORKETH PATIENCE. But let patience have her perfect work, that ye may be perfect and entire, wanting nothing." (James 1:2-4)

"For what glory is it, if, when ye be buffeted for your faults, ye shall take it patiently? but if, when ye do well, and suffer for it, YE TAKE IT PATIENTLY, this is acceptable with God." (1 Peter 2:20)

"Of course, you get no credit for being patient if you are beaten for doing wrong. But if you suffer for doing good and ENDURE IT PATIENTLY, God is pleased with you." (1 Peter 2:20 NLT)

We are a church of FAITH.

"Then said David to the Philistine, Thou comest to me with a sword, and with a spear, and with a shield: but I come to thee in the name of the LORD of hosts, the God of the armies of Israel, whom thou hast defied. This day will the LORD deliver thee into mine hand; and I will smite thee, and take thine head from thee; and I will give the carcases of the host of the Philistines this day unto the fowls of the air, and to the wild beasts of the earth; that all the earth may know that there is a God in Israel. and all this assembly shall know that the LORD saveth not with sword and spear: for the battle is the LORD'S, and he will give you into our hands." (1 Samuel 17:45-47)

"And his name [Jesus] THROUGH FAITH IN HIS NAME hath made this man strong, whom ye see and know: yea, THE FAITH WHICH IS BY HIM hath given him this perfect soundness in the presence of you all." (Acts 3:16)

"For therein is the righteousness of God revealed from faith to faith: as it is written, The just shall live BY FAITH." (Romans 1:17)

"(For we walk BY FAITH, not by sight:)" (2 Corinthians 5:7)

"That Christ may dwell in your hearts BY FAITH; that ye, being rooted and grounded in love," (Ephesians 3:17)

"But WITHOUT FAITH it is impossible to please him: for he that cometh to God must believe that he is, and that he is a rewarder of them that diligently seek him." (Hebrews 11:6)

We (the church) DO NOT take revenge.

"After Saul had left the cave and gone on his way, David came out and shouted after him, 'My lord the king!' And when Saul looked around, David bowed low before him. Then he shouted to Saul, 'Why do you listen to the people who say I am trying to harm you? This very day you can see with your own eyes it isn't true. For the Lord placed you at my mercy back there in the cave. Some of my men told me to kill you, but I spared you. For I said, 'I will never harm the king—he is the lord's anointed one.' Look, my father, at what I have in my hand. It is a piece of the hem of your robe! I cut it off, but I didn't kill you … MAY THE LORD JUDGE BETWEEN US. Perhaps the LORD WILL PUNISH YOU for what you are trying to do to me, but I will never harm you …" (1 Samuel 24:9-12 NLT)

"Dearly beloved, AVENGE NOT yourselves, but rather give place unto wrath: for it is written, Vengeance is mine; I will repay, saith the Lord." (Romans 12:19)

We (the church) must GUARD (watch over) what we say.

"GUARD YOUR WORDS and you'll guard your life, but if you don't control your tongue, it will ruin everything." (Proverbs 13:13 TPT)

"Guard your words, MIND WHAT YOU SAY, and you will keep yourself out of trouble." (Proverbs 21:23 VOICE)

"Suffer not thy mouth to cause thy flesh to sin." (Ecclesiastes 5:6)

"Don't let your mouth get you in trouble!" (Ecclesiastes 5:6 CEV)

"Let NO CORRUPT COMMUNICATION proceed out of your mouth, but that which is good to the use of edifying, that it may minister grace unto the hearers." (Ephesians 4:29)

"Out of the same mouth proceedeth blessing and cursing. My brethren, these things ought not so to be. Doth a fountain send forth at the same place sweet water and bitter? Can the fig tree, my brethren, bear olive berries? either a vine, figs? so can no fountain both yield salt water and fresh." (James 3:10-12)

"For BY THY WORDS thou shalt be justified, and BY THY WORDS thou shalt be condemned." (James 3:37)

We are a gentle (respectful) church.

"So then, my fellow believers, when you assemble as one to share a meal, SHOW RESPECT for one another and wait for all to be served." (1 Corinthians 11:33 TPT)

"Love is GENTLE and consistently kind to all." (1 Corinthians 13:4 TPT)

"But the fruit produced by the Holy Spirit within you is divine love in all its varied expressions: joy that overflows, peace that subdues, patience that endures, kindness in action, a life full of virtue, faith that prevails, GENTLENESS OF HEART, and strength of spirit. Never set the law above these qualities, for they are meant to be limitless." (Galatians 5:22-23 TPT)

"My beloved friends, if you see a believer who is overtaken with a fault, may the one who overflows with the Spirit seek to restore him. Win him over WITH GENTLE WORDS, which will open his heart to you and will keep you from exalting yourself over him." (Galatians 6:1 TPT)

"BE GENTLE and humble, unoffendable in your patience with others." (Colossians 3:12 TPT)

"For lasting beauty comes from a GENTLE AND PEACEFUL SPIRIT, which is precious in God's sight and is much more important than the outward adornment of elaborate hair, jewelry, and fine clothes." (1 Peter 3:3-4 TPT)

"But dedicate your lives to Christ as Lord. always be ready to defend your confidence in God when anyone asks you to explain it. However, make your defense WITH GENTLENESS AND RESPECT. Keep your conscience clear. Then those who treat the good Christian life you live with contempt will feel ashamed that they have ridiculed you."(1 Peter 3:15-16 GW)

Our (the church) response to anything or anyone is PRAYER.

"But I say unto you, Love your enemies, bless them that curse you, do good to them that hate you, and PRAY FOR THEM which despitefully use you, and persecute you; That ye may be the children of your Father which is in heaven: for he maketh his sun to rise on the evil and on the good, and sendeth rain on the just and on the unjust." (Matthew 5:44-45)

"I exhort therefore, that, first of all, supplications, PRAYERS, intercessions, and giving of thanks, be made for all men; For kings, and for all that are in authority; that we may lead a quiet and peaceable life in all godliness and honesty. For this is good and acceptable in the sight of God our Saviour."
(1 Timothy 2:1-3)

"Confess your faults one to another, and PRAY ONE FOR ANOTHER, that ye may be healed. The effectual fervent prayer of a righteous man availeth much." (James 5:16)
"PRAY without ceasing." (1 Thessalonians 5:17)

"But ye, beloved, building up yourselves on your most holy faith, PRAYING IN THE HOLY GHOST, Keep yourselves in the love of God, looking for the mercy of our Lord Jesus Christ unto eternal life. And of some have compassion, making a difference: And others save with fear, pulling them out of the fire; hating even the garment spotted by the flesh." (Jude 1:20-23)

We (the church) must accompany our prayers with PRAISE and GIVING THANKS.

"I will bless the LORD at all times: HIS PRAISE shall CONTINUALLY be in my mouth." (Psalm 34:1)

"And at midnight Paul and Silas prayed, and SANG PRAISES unto God: and the prisoners heard them." (Acts 16:25)

"I exhort therefore, that, first of all, supplications, prayers, intercessions, AND GIVING OF THANKS, be made for all men; For kings, and for all that are in authority; that we may lead a quiet and peaceable life in all godliness and honesty. For this is good and acceptable in the sight of God our Saviour." (1 Timothy 2:1-3)

"REJOICE evermore. Pray without ceasing. In EVERY THING GIVE THANKS: for this is the will of God in Christ Jesus concerning you." (1 Thessalonians 5:16-18)

We (the church) are a SHARING church. The harvest must be shared with others.

"If a fellow Hebrew sells himself or herself to be your servant and serves you for six years, in the seventh year you must set that servant free. When you release a male servant, DO NOT SEND HIM AWAY EMPTY-HANDED. Give him a generous farewell gift from your flock, your threshing floor, and your winepress. SHARE WITH HIM SOME OF THE BOUNTY with which the Lord your God has blessed you. Remember that you were once slaves in the land of Egypt and the Lord your God redeemed you! That is why I am giving you this command." (Deuteronomy 15:12-15 NLT)

"He continued, 'Go home and prepare a feast, holiday food and drink; AND SHARE IT with those who don't have anything: This day is holy to God. Don't feel bad. The joy of God is your strength!'" (Nehemiah 8:10 MSG)

"Learn to GENEROUSLY SHARE what you have with those who ask for help, and don't close your heart to the one who comes to borrow from you." (Matthew 5:42 TPT)

"Go out into the world AND SHARE the good news with all of creation." (Mark 16:15 VOICE)

"And he [Jesus] spake a parable unto them, saying, The ground of a certain rich man brought forth plentifully: And he thought within himself, saying, What shall I do, because I have no room where to bestow my fruits? And he said, This will I do: I will pull down my barns, and build greater; and there will I bestow all my fruits and my goods. And I will say to my soul, Soul, thou hast much goods laid up for many years; take thine ease, eat, drink, and be merry. but God said unto him, Thou fool, this night thy soul shall be required of thee: then whose shall those things be, which thou hast provided? SO IS HE THAT LAYETH UP TREASURE FOR HIMSELF, AND IS NOT RICH TOWARD GOD." (Luke 12:16-21)
"Daily they met together in the temple courts and in one another's homes to celebrate communion. They SHARED meals together with joyful hearts and tender humility." (Acts 2:46 TPT)

We (the church) are SUBMISSIVE (give honor) to government (leadership).

"And when they were come to Capernaum, they that received tribute money came to Peter, and said, Doth not your master pay tribute? He saith, Yes. And when he was come into the house, Jesus prevented him, saying, What thinkest thou, Simon? of whom do the kings of the earth take custom or tribute? of their own children, or of strangers? Peter saith unto him, Of strangers. Jesus saith unto him, Then are the children free. Notwithstanding, LEST WE SHOULD OFFEND THEM, go thou to the sea, and cast an hook, and take up the fish that first cometh up; and when thou hast opened his mouth, thou shalt find a piece of money: that take, and give unto them for me and thee." (Matthew 17:24-27)

"But Jesus perceived their wickedness, and said, Why tempt ye me, ye hypocrites? Shew me the tribute money. And they brought unto him a penny. And he saith unto them, Whose is this image and superscription? They say unto him, Caesar's. Then saith he unto them, RENDER THEREFORE UNTO CAESAR THE THINGS WHICH ARE CAESAR'S*; and unto God the things that are God's."* (Matthew 22:18-21)

"Let every soul be subject unto the HIGHER POWERS. For there is no power but of God: THE POWERS THAT BE ARE ORDAINED OF GOD. Whosoever therefore RESISTETH THE POWER, RESISTETH THE ORDINANCE OF GOD: and they that resist shall receive to themselves damnation." (Romans 13:1-2)

"It is important that all of us SUBMIT to the authorities who have charge over us because GOD ESTABLISHES ALL AUTHORITY IN HEAVEN AND ON THE EARTH. Therefore, a person who rebels against authority rebels against the order He established, and people like that can expect to face certain judgment. You see, if you do the right thing, you have nothing to be worried about from the rulers; but if you do what you know is wrong, the rulers will make sure you pay a price. Would you not rather live with a clear conscience than always have to be looking over your shoulder? Then keep doing what you know to be good and right, and they will publicly honor you ... SO SUBMISSION IS NOT OPTIONAL; IT'S REQUIRED. But don't just submit for the sake of avoiding punishment; SUBMIT AND ABIDE BY THE LAWS BECAUSE YOUR CONSCIENCE LEADS YOU TO DO THE RIGHT THING. Pay your taxes for the same reason because the authorities are servants of God, giving their full attention to take care of these things. Pay all of them what you owe. If you owe taxes, then pay. If you owe fees, then pay. In the same way, GIVE HONOR AND RESPECT TO THOSE WHO DESERVE IT." (Romans 13:1-7 VOICE)

"That's also why you pay taxes—so that an orderly way of life can be maintained. Fulfill your obligations as a citizen. Pay your taxes, pay your bills, RESPECT YOUR LEADERS." (Romans 13:6-7 MSG)

"SUBMIT YOURSELVES TO EVERY ORDINANCE OF MAN for the Lord's sake: whether it be to the king, as supreme; Or unto governors, as unto them that are sent by him for the punishment of evildoers, and for the praise of them that do well. For so is the will of God, that WITH WELL DOING ye may put to silence the ignorance of foolish men: As free, and NOT USING YOUR LIBERTY FOR A CLOKE OF MALICIOUSNESS,

but as THE SERVANTS OF GOD. Honour all men. Love the brotherhood. Fear God. Honour the king." (1 Peter 2:13-17)

"In order to honor the Lord, you must RESPECT and DEFER to the authority of every human institution, whether it be the highest ruler or the governors he puts in place to punish lawbreakers and to praise those who do what's right. For it is God's will for you to silence the ignorance of foolish people by DOING WHAT IS RIGHT." (1 Peter 2:13-15 TPT)

"Those who are servants, submit to the authority of those who are your masters—not only to those who are kind and gentle but EVEN TO THOSE WHO ARE HARD AND DIFFICULT. You find God's favor by DECIDING TO PLEASE GOD even when you endure hardships because of unjust suffering." (1 Peter 2:18-19 TPT)

We (the church) pray and give thanks for our leaders.

"During these years of captivity, let your families grow and not die out. PURSUE THE PEACE AND WELFARE OF THE CITY where I sent you into exile. PRAY TO ME, THE ETERNAL, FOR BABYLON because if it has peace, you will live in peace.'" (Jeremiah 29:6-7 VOICE)

"I exhort therefore, that, first of all, SUPPLICATIONS, PRAYERS, INTERCESSIONS, and GIVING OF THANKS, be made for all men; FOR KINGS, AND FOR ALL THAT ARE IN AUTHORITY; that we may lead a quiet and peaceable life in all godliness and honesty. For this is good and acceptable in the sight of God our Saviour." (1 Timothy 2:1-3)

We are the OBEDIENT church. We are NOT rebellious.

"And Samuel said, Hath the LORD as great delight in burnt offerings and sacrifices, as in OBEYING the voice of the LORD? Behold, TO OBEY IS BETTER than sacrifice, and to hearken than the fat of rams. FOR REBELLION IS AS THE SIN OF WITCHCRAFT, AND STUBBORNNESS IS AS INIQUITY AND IDOLATRY. Because thou hast rejected the word of the LORD, he hath also rejected thee from being king." (1 Samuel 15:22-23)

"An evil man seeketh only rebellion." (Proverbs 17:11)

"If ye be WILLING AND OBEDIENT, ye shall eat the good of the land: But if ye refuse and rebel, ye shall be devoured with the sword: for the mouth of the LORD hath spoken it." (Isaiah 1:19-20)

"Know ye not that the unrighteous shall not inherit the kingdom of God? Be not deceived: neither fornicators, nor IDOLATERS, nor adulterers, nor effeminate, nor abusers of themselves with mankind, Nor thieves, nor covetous, nor drunkards, nor revilers, nor extortioners, shall inherit the kingdom of God." (1 Corinthians 6:9-10)

"Now the works of the flesh are manifest, which are these; Adultery, fornication, uncleanness, lasciviousness, IDOLATRY, WITCHCRAFT, hatred, variance, emulations, wrath, strife, seditions, heresies, Envyings, murders, drunkenness, revellings, and such like: of the which I tell you before, as I have also told you in time past, that they which do such things shall not inherit the kingdom of God." (Galatians 5:19-21)

We are a PEACEFUL church.

"Depart from evil, and do good; SEEK PEACE, and pursue it." (Psalms 34:14)

"During these years of captivity, let your families grow and not die out. PURSUE THE PEACE AND WELFARE OF THE CITY where I sent you into exile. pray to me, the eternal, for Babylon because if it has peace, you will live in peace.'" (Jeremiah 29:6-7 VOICE)

"FOLLOW PEACE with all men, and holiness, without which no man shall see the Lord: Looking diligently lest any man fail of the grace of God; lest any root of bitterness springing up trouble you, and thereby many be defiled." (Hebrews 12:14-15)

"But the wisdom that is from above is first pure, then PEACEABLE, gentle, and easy to be intreated, full of mercy and good fruits, without partiality, and without hypocrisy. And the fruit of righteousness is sown in peace of THEM THAT MAKE PEACE." (James 3:17-18)

"For lasting beauty comes from a GENTLE AND PEACEFUL SPIRIT, which is precious in God's sight and is much more important than the outward adornment of elaborate hair, jewelry, and fine clothes." (1 Peter 3:3-4 TPT)

"Let him eschew evil, and do good; let him SEEK PEACE, and ensue it." (1 Peter 3:11)

We are a TITHING (giving) church.

"And blessed be the most high God, which hath delivered thine enemies into thy hand. And he gave him tithes of all." (Genesis 14:20)

"And this stone, which I have set for a pillar, shall be God's house: and of all that thou shalt give me I will surely give the tenth unto thee." (Genesis 28:22)

"And all the tithe of the land, whether of the seed of the land, or of the fruit of the tree, is the LORD'S: it is holy unto the LORD." (Leviticus 27:30)

"Honour the LORD with thy substance, and with the firstfruits of all thine increase: So shall thy barns be filled with plenty, and thy presses shall burst out with new wine." (Proverbs 3:9-10)

"But when thou doest alms, let not thy left hand know what thy right hand doeth: That thine alms may be in secret: and thy Father which seeth in secret himself shall reward thee openly." (Matthew 6:3-4)

"Sell that ye have, and give alms; provide yourselves bags which wax not old, a treasure in the heavens that faileth not, where no thief approacheth, neither moth corrupteth. For where your treasure is, there will your heart be also." (Luke 12:33-34)

"And he said, Of a truth I say unto you, that this poor widow hath cast in more than they all: For all these have of their abundance cast in unto the offerings of God: but she of her penury hath cast in all the living that she had." (Luke 21:3-4)

We (the church) are CHEERFUL (not grudging) givers.

"And Abel, he also brought of the firstlings of his flock and of the fat thereof. And the LORD had respect unto Abel and to his offering: But unto Cain and to his offering he had not respect. And Cain was very wroth, and his countenance fell." (Genesis 4:4-5)

"Will a man rob God? Yet ye have robbed me. But ye say, Wherein have we robbed thee? In tithes and offerings. Ye are cursed with a curse: for ye have robbed me, even this whole nation. Bring ye all the tithes into the storehouse, that there may be meat in mine house, and prove me now herewith, saith the LORD of hosts, if I will not open you the windows of heaven, and pour you out a blessing, that there shall not be room enough to receive it." (Malachi 3:8-10)

"Judge not, and ye shall not be judged: condemn not, and ye shall not be condemned: forgive, and ye shall be forgiven: Give, and it shall be given unto you; good measure, pressed down, and shaken together, and running over, shall men give into your bosom. For with the same measure that ye mete withal it shall be measured to you again." (Luke 6:37-38)

"And he looked up, and saw the rich men casting their gifts into the treasury. And he saw also a certain poor widow casting in thither two mites. And he said, Of a truth I say unto you, that this poor widow hath cast in more than they all: For all these have of their abundance cast in unto the offerings of God: but she of her penury hath cast in all the living that she had." (Luke 21:1-4)

"Every man according as he purposeth in his heart, so let him give; NOT GRUDGINGLY, or of necessity: for God loveth A CHEERFUL GIVER." (2 Corinthians 9:2)

We (the church) are faithful STEWARDS of God's money. He is the OWNER.

"And the Lord said, Who then is that FAITHFUL AND WISE STEWARD, whom his lord shall make ruler over his household, to give them their portion of meat in due season?" (Luke 12:42)

"If you're FAITHFUL in small-scale matters, you'll be FAITHFUL with far bigger responsibilities. If you're crooked in small responsibilities, you'll be no different in bigger things. If you can't even handle a small thing like money, who's going to entrust you with spiritual riches that really matter? If you don't manage well someone else's assets that are entrusted to you, who's going to give over to you important spiritual and personal relationships to manage?" (Luke 16:10-12 VOICE)

"Imagine you're a servant and you have two masters giving you orders. What are you going to do when they have conflicting demands? You can't serve both, so you'll either hate the first and love the second, or you'll faithfully serve the first and despise the second. One master is god and the other is money. You can't serve them both." (Lk 16:13 VOICE)

"Moreover it is required in stewards, that a man be found FAITHFUL." (1 Corinthians 4:2)

We are a GENEROUS church.

"But if there are any poor Israelites in your towns when you arrive in the land the Lord your God is giving you, DO NOT BE HARD-HEARTED OR TIGHTFISTED toward them. Instead, BE GENEROUS and lend them whatever they need. DO NOT BE MEAN-SPIRITED and refuse someone a loan because the year for canceling debts is close at hand. If you refuse to make the loan and the needy person cries out to the Lord, you will be considered guilty of sin. GIVE GENEROUSLY to the poor, NOT GRUDGINGLY, for the Lord your God will bless you in everything you do." (Deuteronomy 15:7-10)

"If a fellow Hebrew sells himself or herself to be your servant and serves you for six years, in the seventh year you must set that servant free. When you release a male servant, DO NOT SEND HIM AWAY EMPTY-HANDED. Give him A GENEROUS FAREWELL GIFT from your flock, your threshing floor, and your winepress. SHARE WITH HIM SOME OF THE BOUNTY with which the Lord your God has blessed you. Remember that you were once slaves in the land of Egypt and the Lord your God redeemed you! That is why I am giving you this command." (Deuteronomy 15:12-15 NLT)

"Ye have heard that it hath been said, An eye for an eye, and a tooth for a tooth: But I say unto you, That ye resist not evil: but whosoever shall smite thee on thy right cheek, TURN TO HIM THE OTHER ALSO. And if any man will sue thee at the law, and take away thy coat, LET HIM HAVE THY CLOKE ALSO. And whosoever shall compel thee to go a mile, GO WITH HIM TWAIN. Give to him that asketh thee, and from him that would borrow of thee turn not thou away." (Matthew 5:38-42)

"If a brother or sister be naked, and destitute of daily food, And one of you say unto them, Depart in peace, be ye warmed and filled; notwithstanding ye give them not those things which are needful to the body; what doth it profit?" (James 2:15-16)

We (the church) are men and women of God.

"But thou, O MAN OF GOD, flee these things; and follow after righteousness, godliness, faith, love, patience, meekness." (1 Timothy 6:11)

"For men shall be lovers of their own selves ... Having a form of godliness, but denying the power thereof: from such turn away." (2 Timothy 3:2, 5)

"All scripture is given by inspiration of God, and is profitable for doctrine, for reproof, for correction, for instruction in righteousness: That the MAN OF GOD may be perfect, throughly furnished unto all good works." (2 Timothy 3:16-17)

We (the church) STAY FILLED with God.

"He will be standing firm like a flourishing tree planted by God's design, deeply rooted by the brooks of bliss, bearing fruit in every season of his life. He IS NEVER DRY, never fainting, ever blessed, ever prosperous." (Psalm 1:3 TPT)

"Thou preparest a table before me in the presence of mine enemies: thou anointest my head with oil; my cup RUNNETH OVER." (Psalms 23:5)

"The Fear-of-God is a spring of LIVING water." (Proverbs 14:27 MSG)

"Let righteousness flow like a mighty river that NEVER RUNS DRY." (Amos 5:24 VOICE)

Jesus answered, 'If you drink from Jacob's well you'll be thirsty again and again, but if anyone drinks the living water I give them, they will never thirst again and will be forever satisfied! For when you drink the water I give you it becomes A GUSHING FOUNTAIN OF THE HOLY SPIRIT, SPRINGING UP AND FLOODING YOU WITH ENDLESS LIFE!'" (Jn 4:13-14 TPT)

"And when the day of Pentecost was fully come, they were all with one accord in one place ... And they were ALL FILLED with the Holy Ghost." (Acts 2:1, 4)

"Then Peter, FILLED with the Holy Ghost, said unto them, Ye rulers of the people, and elders of Israel." (Acts 4:8)

"And when they had prayed, the place was shaken where they were assembled together; and they were all FILLED with the Holy Ghost, and they spake the word of God with boldness." (Acts 4:29-31)

"And [God] hath put all things under his [Christ's] feet, and gave him to be the head over all things to the church, Which is his body, the FULNESS OF HIM THAT FILLETH all in all." (Ephesians 1:22-23)

"And to know the love of Christ, which passeth knowledge, that ye might be FILLED with all the fulness of God." (Ephesians 3:19)

"And be not drunk with wine, wherein is excess; but BE FILLED with the Spirit." (Ephesians 5:18)

"And he said unto me, It is done. I am Alpha and Omega, the beginning and the end. I will give unto him that is athirst of the fountain of the water of life freely." (Revelation 21:6)

We (the church) LIVE and WALK in the Spirit of God.

"This I say then, Walk in the Spirit, and ye shall not fulfil the lust of the flesh." (Galatians 5:16)

"If we live in the Spirit, let us also walk in the Spirit." (Galatians 5:25)

The Car Analogy

The car is: the device that moves us forward.

The fuel is: being continually filled with the Holy Spirit.

The engine is: DUNAMIS, the POWER of GOD'S NATURE, His EXCELLENCE, and MIGHT.

The gas pedal is: prayer.

The key is: faith.

The spark is : walking in love with our neighbor and being in submission.

The driver's license is: only obtained through salvation.

The door is: Jesus.

The music is: our praises.

The devil has no place in the car unless we let him in. Offense and criticism are like putting diesel fuel in an unleaded gasoline engine.

About The Author

Author, Suzanne D. Williams, is a native Floridian, wife, mother, and photographer. She is the author of both nonfiction and fiction books. She writes devotionals and instructional articles for various blogs. She also does graphic design for self-publishing authors.

She is free of fear. She is obedient to God's Word. She is blessed.

For more information or to contact Suzanne, visit her website **www.suzannedwilliams.com**

Other *Christian Living* books by this author

Fearless
(Testimonial Book)

Conversations with God
(Free at all retailers)

A Good Life: A Daily Walk in God's Presence

Other books published by Becky Combee Ministries, Inc.
www.beckycombeeministries.com

This Is Love
Healing: More Than A Theory